Exploration
Into
God

Life is only for love
Time is only that we may find God

St. Bernard

Exploration Into God

George Trevelyan

GATEWAY BOOKS BATH | 1991

First published in 1991
by Gateway Books
The Hollies, Wellow
Bath BA2 8QJ

Set in Palatino
by Ann Buchan (Typesetters), Middlesex
Printed and bound by Billings of Worcester
Cover design by Paul Nelson

British Library Cataloguing in Publication Data:
A catalogue record for this book is
available from the British Library

Contents

Foreword

THIS BOOK, third of a trilogy, follows *A Vision of the Aquarian Age* and *Operation Redemption*. As I worked on it, I suddenly knew that its title must be "Exploration into God". What presumption I thought! Who am I, who have no qualifications whatever as a theologian, to use such a title? Yet I knew it was right and fitting. The phrase comes from a passage in Christopher Fry's play "A Sleep of Prisoners". Prisoners of war, locked in an empty church at night (itself a powerful symbol) talk and banter, joke and smoke, but one after another they are taken over and speak from higher inspiration out of the spiritual world. Finally Meadows, the Sergeant, touched with the higher consciousness, says this:

> *The human heart can go the lengths of God.*
> *Dark and cold we may be, but this*
> *Is no winter now. The frozen misery*
> *of centuries breaks, cracks, begins to move;*
> *The thunder is the thunder of the floes,*
> *The thaw, the flood, the upstart Spring.*
> *Thank God our Time is now when wrong*
> *Comes up to face us everywhere,*
> *Never leave us till we take*
> *The longest stride of soul men ever took.*
> *Affairs are now soul size.*
> *The enterprise*
> *Is exploration into God.*
> *Where are you making for? It takes*
> *So many thousand years to wake*
> *But will you wake for pity's sake?*

I have quoted this frequently in lectures, since it gives a powerful expression of the age we live in and the hope of a change in consciousness which will usher in a New Age.

While Principal of Attingham Park, I invited a distinguished theologian and Shakespearean scholar to conduct a weekend course on the work of Christopher Fry. I spoke of my admiration of the above passage and to my great surprise he responded:

> Oh, Christopher went badly wrong there! There can be no question of our exploring into God. All we can do is to pray and wait for God's grace to be granted to us.

And then I saw that the emergence of the spiritual and holistic world-view in our time was calling and challenging us to go beyond academic or traditional viewpoints and really take our own initiative in exploring into the field of God-thought. So I offer it, with due humility, as truth.

The Enterprise is Exploration into God.

PART I

Vision of Hope

A Letter to the Reader

Dear READER,

I greet you. This letter is written to you, for you. I do not know you—or do I? We are linked by the mere fact of your opening this book. And because, on the deeper, higher, grander level, we are all parts of one stupendous Whole, an awakening being, called Humanity. Through us both pulsates the flow of life. We are alive. And life axiomatically is something which cannot die. It makes no sense to think it can be extinguished. We experience ourselves as a being of life, inhabiting a very astonishing structure of sensitivity and capacity called a body. Think imaginatively. Start from here.

If you are young, then I urge you to see, with courage, that you are incarnated in perhaps the most dramatic and exciting period and generation in human history. If you, like me, are of advancing years, then look forward with keen anticipation to what may come after your release and realise that the present period of alarms and disturbances is one of transition and cleansing of the planet at the opening of a new age. We each of us have a part to play in this cosmic drama.

We are called on to change our thinking. "Change your thinking, for the Kingdom of Heaven is at hand within you." That is the clarion call, given two thousand years ago by Him who now overlights the great transition into a new epoch. "Repent" as it is usually translated, gives the wrong connotation. The Greek word was *Metanoia*, which implies deliberate change in our thinking. Here's the challenge.

Let me say again what I find so necessary to repeat. In no sense is this dogma which you are meant to believe. Nobody is forcing anything on you. If you don't chime with it, drop it, bless you. The New Age is not a proselytizing religious cult. We are called on to explore into the realm of living divine ideas. This is a stage of breakthrough for the human mind. Let's try to summarise it.

The basic concept is that the thing in you and me which can say "I" is a droplet of divinity, a spark of God, housed temporarily in a body in order to experience lessons of creative freedom which only Earth can teach. Now, I can't prove that. It is an idea. The critical intellect can demand proof before accepting it. But spiritual ideas can't be proven in the way science studies facts. The spirit bloweth where it listeth.

We are challenged to think ideas which we cannot prove intellectually. Now let me offer a technique vital for our entry into the Aquarian Age. Do please master it.

You obviously recognise in yourself the faculty of apprehending an idea for its excitement and beauty. You can seize it out of the ether and look at it—like a beautiful butterfly or blossom. It may give a new flash of understanding or point out a path of courageous action. Then how often cold intellect steps in and says "Oh no you don't! You can't prove that; and your scientific training tells you that you may not believe anything you can't weigh and measure with the senses. Anyway, if you follow that course, people will think you silly and you have an important engagement next Thursday! So drop it."

Alas, and you let the butterfly fly away.

> *Thus conscience does make cowards of us all*
> *And thus the native hue of resolution*
> *Is sicklied o'er by the pale cast of thought*
> *And enterprises of great pith and moment*
> *With this regard their currents turn awry*
> *And lose the name of action.*

Thus spoke Hamlet,

Now, listen. Our task is to learn how to think spiritual ideas and act on them, even though you *cannot* prove them. Awaken the intuitive faculty. Acknowledge that you have this inner power of apprehending a beautiful idea. Take it. Love it. Put it in your heart and thinking, and decide to live for a week *as if you believed it*, while reserving judgement. *Act as if you believed it* and watch what happens.

Take, for instance, that superb idea, that you are an imperishable droplet of God. If it is true, then the implications, as we shall find in later chapters, are immense and endless. It would open on to a path of thrilling exploration. Don't wait to prove it first. Plunge in and act as if it were true, neither believing nor disbelieving, but trying it out. 'Act as if', and watch the result. Such an idea is *alive*. It is truly a being, a living strand in the thought of God. (That, incidentally, is another idea, initially unprovable, but work with it.)

A living idea will, if true, draw certainty to itself as you live with it. If untrue (or untrue to you) it will fade out. Anyway, as you live out such an idea and really act the part, you must inevitably become a more courageous, tolerant, tolerable, loving, compassionate person: Everybody gains and nothing is lost by the trying. By exploring into ideas and living with them we get subjective proof, and we can all find it. But we need never demand acceptance or belief.

The 'I' in you is alive. Axiomatically this point of life is immortal, for life cannot possibly be extinguished, whatever happens to its temporary sheath of an ageing body. Therefore it was from the beginning, is now and ever more shall be. What a conception! You are a droplet of consciousness in that eternal ocean of life, one with the Whole, yet with identity. Of course you survive! How could you do other? The far more important implication is *pre-existence*—that you were there before you were born, an already developed entity coming down into embodiment for a purpose.

Thus we leap to the concept of the Planet Earth as the training ground for souls, the school for evolving consciousness. It would be ridiculous to think you could qualify to enter the university by dropping into the third form for one term. We see that Earth is a living, breathing, thinking being, an organism with its own evolving consciousness, carrying this precious cargo of self-consciousness which we call humanity. So we see that we must surely have passed through all the school grades to learn the lessons which Earth alone can teach. Repeated Earth lives emerges as an essential concept. The readiness to think reincarnation (and live as if it were true) spreads now through our society and for many becomes axiomatic. How it enriches our sense of meaning in life! Look at your relatives, your friends, and those you meet and feel the sudden gush of recognition in their eyes. Souls are finding each other again. There is purpose in it all, and meaning. The droplet of life which is you, must be going through its experiences as a long training, and humanity is seen as a living tapestry of inter-connection.

Now let's follow where the idea leads us. Look into the eyes of another human being. Normally only lovers or children can do this. It is too shy-making. But agree to cut out personality reactions. No need to smile or respond or talk. Just gaze into the human eye, thinking that the God in me is looking at the God spark in you. But it is the same God, looking at Himself and wondering what has happened to that particle of Himself. If I look at you in this way I experience that we are both parts of the same vast being that is the totality of humanity. I cannot hurt you or insult you, murder you or talk scandal about you, for I know I should be hurting myself. I love you as part of myself.

We are learning that we are each a cell in the great body of humanity. This letter is written to you who are feeling your way into the new understanding that all is One. To ever more people this holistic world-view becomes acceptable. It is an awakening which brings with it a deeper meaning to life and purpose for living. Humankind now stands at the threshold when this change in vision has become possible. Open your thinking to it. Lift beyond the merely sensory interpretation of the world around us. The senses initially tell us that we are separate entities among an infinite number of separate things. Now into our intuitive, imaginative thinking seeps and floods the realization that everything—EVERY THING— is inter-connected and flows into everything else in a vast living pattern.

Humanity is waking up. We discover that we have subtler senses which can apprehend the oneness of all things. It offers a new world to explore. And not only intellectually. It implies our becoming a new kind of person—and a kinder person, for "we needs must love the highest when we see it". We are working to open the eye of the mind—the all-seeing eye.

This book, I know, is saying only what is obvious to so many awakened souls. Many are writing books which go far deeper into the new understanding. I am concerned with the awakening from the sleep of the senses. The waking bell is sounding. Wake up. The new day dawns and we have an adventure before us. Will you come?

You can easily grasp that Planet Earth is a living wholeness. Take possession of the idea that Terra is a living creature, of great complexity, but One, and alive. Wherever you start to observe, you find that apparently separate things all inter-connect. The most advanced scientific thinking establishes this. You and I must work with imaginative vision to make good this thought. But already we can feel that our consciousness can take hold of things and apprehend their inter-connection.

The word 'holism' comes into general use. It is defined thus in the Oxford English Dictionary:

> *The tendency in nature to produce wholes from the ordered grouping of units.*

The first thing is to recognise this tendency. It was first put forward by General Smutz in 1927 in his book *Holism and Evolution*. But this still allows for an essentially materialistic world-view: things as they evolve growing and inter-connecting into greater wholes—an impulse which does not need God.

The leap we are making is to conceive that *from the beginning* all was One, the living idea in that great mind and source we call God. By Him all things were made and without Him was not anything made that was made. In Him was Light and the Light was the Life of Man. Grapple with the idea of Oneness with your mind. Holism, wholeness and holiness and health are all one.

Teach yourself to look in a new way. Look behind, through, within and see that every tree and rock, every flower and bird, is an expression (pressing out) of the primal realm of Divine Idea—the primordial Whole. Mind is the endless realm of these ideas which ultimately are ONE IDEA.

Brain is a miraculously complex and wonderful organ enabling us, as spiritual beings, to become conscious of this living Oneness while we are still embodied in matter. Wake up. Take hold of the IDEA within whatever you see.

Here's a lovely little passage from Elizabeth Barrett Browning:

> Earth's crammed with Heaven
> And every common bush afire with God,
> But only he who sees takes off his shoes.
> The rest sit round it and pluck blackberries.

So here's the adventure into wholeness, the awakening of humankind to apprehend the God idea wherever we look, smell, taste, listen and feel. It offers a different approach to Nature, which we shall develop later.

Think big. See Planet Earth as a living orb, very beautiful, a sublime work of art and design, carrying a point of consciousness unlimited, the crowning Mind of humankind. See this turning planet floating in the endless ocean of life and light. Conceive an ocean of thought which is also Love, which holds and imbues every living particle in its cosmic dance. Apprehend that which seems to the cruder senses to be empty space is really total Life, filled with ever subtler forms and ranges of being and beings.

We get a conception of what Jacob's ladder really implies. Jacob had the inner vision of the angels climbing up and down this ladder that leads to Heaven. Grasp that this refers to ever subtler, more refined and rarified levels of being and *frequency*, planes of different and faster vibration. The five major senses are attuned to apprehend the material plane. Thus the subtler planes are invisible to us, so long as we only use the sense vision. But the inner senses can 'see' and apprehend these subtler planes, which are everywhere, but within and within and within. How do we move in and through? This is the new power of observation we have to develop. It is poetical, intuitive, imaginative. We talk of 'higher planes' and it is almost impossible not to make the hand gesture of up and up. But Jacob's ladder really implies passing in and through to higher frequencies *which are all everywhere.* We accept that this room is shot through with an infinite number of wave bands of music and colour, rock and Beethoven, picture and drama quite invisible till we switch on radio or TV. Yet the brain is, we see, the most fabulous of all computers, and is the gateway to the ocean of Mind. Through it we move into realms of wonder or terror or endless interest and vision. Let us learn to explore and to apprehend the IDEA behind all things.

This room is not only shot through with radio waves, but contains God and the angelic world. They are *not* far away beyond the stars. God is everywhere, for God is Life. Life is God. Wherever you apprehend life, there is God. All beings in the angelic realms are aspects of God. The nine angelic hierarchies are God in action.

Augustine wrote:

> *Things were rather in the Angelic Mind than in Nature—that is to say that the Angels perceived and knew all things in their thoughts before they could spring into actual existence. God never works but through them.*

Allow the faculty of imagination to expand and reach out and apprehend the endless ocean of divine energy which is God-thought poured out. An ocean of thought—and of life, pouring ever-new from the Source. The angels, as we have said, are strands of this living thought-energy. Naturally they serve God. How can they do other, for they are Him, and exist to fulfil his grand design and plan?

Out of primal creation in the spiritual universe, the realms of matter and substance come into being, through the lowering of the frequency rate from that excessively high vibration of the spiritual sun, into the low vibration of the visible world of solid matter which we occupy.

Humanity, called the Tenth Hierarchy "a little lower than the angels but crowned with glory and honour", has a very special purpose. The plan is to evolve a being who can go through the (apparent) separation from God, be allowed to forget Him, to flounder in the realm of desire and sensation, to err through the temptations of ego-consciousness and to fall to the seductions which the fallen angels use to misguide him/her.

The great and clear purpose is that Man, the individual soul, male and female in nature, should of free-will and choice come back to God, rediscover His perpetual presence, lift up the frequency bands out of the morass of heavy matter and selfish desire, and of free choice re-dedicate self to working with God, becoming veritably a friend and companion of God, a co-creator.

Planet Earth is seen as the setting of this most astonishing experiment. And now, at the threshold of the Aquarian Age, we enter the culminating years and days when the symbolic inflooding and outpouring of the waters of Aquarius are washing away the old barriers and structures which separate humanity, since anything and everything can change.

So we are urged to wake up and think big, and see that beyond the time of cleansing is the supreme possibility (and certainty) of an age when the golden light of God Life can once again enter our consciousness, and we can individually, and of free choice, blend in thought and love with the beings of the worlds of light.

Blend. Unite. Become one. Surrender and submit. Lift beyond

ego desire. Consciously re-dedicate all that we are to the supreme adventure of becoming ourselves a strand of that ocean of life and divine thought. For this we have gone through the aeons of evolution and have now in these immediate years reached the culmination point when we can awaken from the long sleep of matter and enter, of conscious choice, on to the next phase of exploration into God.

This is the divine adventure. Each of us is given totally free choice at this dividing of the ways. Do we choose to throw ourselves on the life and power divine, and call upon our angel guides, grasping the quite endless possibilities of adventure, change and development into a new Golden Age? Or do we prefer to reject this and go on gratifying the desires of ego, experiencing separation, allowing fear, greed, desire for power and all the emotions which lead to violence to dominate our lives?

There is no constraint. It is not a question of sheep and goats, the elite or the rejected. The choice is for each of us, for humanity is called and invited to take:

> *The longest stride of soul men ever took*
> *Affairs are now soul size*
> *The enterprise*
> *is exploration into God.*
> *Where are you making for?*
> *It takes so many thousand years to wake,*
> *But will you wake, for pity's sake!*

(Christopher Fry)

What then is the path forward?

Change your thinking, for the Kingdom of Heaven is within you.

I AM with you always, even to the end of the world, closer than breathing, nearer than hands and feet.

What can be nearer than breathing? Clearly only our think-ing. *Within our own thinking* we can learn to hear God and our angel guides. This is the great and wonderful challenge for each of us.

Now we see how the design inherent in the evolutionary impulse has produced within nature an organ of consciousness through which the human being can lift self into Greater Self. The human brain, separated into its two halves, is the organ through which intellect can lift into INTELLIGENCE.

Left hemisphere, masculine intellect, sees separation of the world into a mass of different things. Right hemisphere, the feminine, poetical faculties which can apprehend the living Whole, can see and know that everything is inter-connected, everything is alive and inter-related. Mind can blend with mind, and consciousness is unlimited and can enter the ocean of thought and life. And Love—for unconditional love is the nature of this Divine Light.

> Feel the self fade, feel the great life begin,
>   with Love re-rising in the cosmic morn.
> The inward ardour yearns to the inmost goal,
> The endless goal is one with the endless way,
>   From every gulf the tides of Being roll,
> From every zenith burns the indwelling day,
>   And life in Life hath drowned thee, soul in Soul
> And these are God, and thou thyself art they.

(F.W. Myers—A Cosmic Outlook)

All this is fine, resounding stuff and easy enough to write! Yet perhaps it is valid to overspill into grandiloquent phrases, since we are each experiencing this breakdown, breakup, break in, BREAKTHROUGH. Here obviously we are in touch with tremendous possibilities which at present are inevitably ignored by our politics, economics and sociology in our attempts to solve insuperable and terrible planetary problems of our own making. Perhaps we are being battered or inspired into recognition that God *is* on the march and that we, each individually, are called on and challenged to take our own courageous step into the unknown.

I said to the man at the gate of the year,
Give me a light that I may move safely into the unknown.
And he said—Go forth into the darkness
* and put your hand into the hand of God.*
That shall be better than a light, and safer than any
* known way.*
So I went forth, and finding the Hand of God, trod gladly
* into the night.*
And He led me towards the hills and the breaking of day in
* the Lone East.*

We call for blessing on the spiritual journey.
Dear Reader, I salute you, companion of the path.

George

I AM · HE/SHE IS · WE ARE ONE

Let me make it abundantly clear that whenever I use the word MAN, I am referring to Genus Homo Sapiens and not merely the male of the species.

It is to be regretted that our language offers the same word for both meanings. It would be clumsy always to write or say male/female or he/she. And we hardly know what to do about "God". Perhaps the early suffragettes had a point when they declared:

We put our trust in God, for we know She is with us!

Of course in this age we must establish that the Human Being is balanced male/female.

New Age thinking assuredly rises above old concepts of male supremacy!

New Consciousness
for a New Future

THE MOST REMARKABLE PHENOMENON in the intellectual climate of our time is the melting of the barriers between science and mysticism. For three centuries the two modes of experiencing reality have flowed in separate streams. Now they begin to merge in the vision of wholeness, the holistic world-view.

It was right and inevitable that thinking in the West should take the plunge into intellectual exploration of the material world. The principle established first by Francis Bacon and developed by Newton was rightly that an experimental science might believe nothing that could not be proven by the senses. Neither of these great thinkers doubted the existence of the divine worlds, but they accepted this principle in order to clear away the clutter of medieval theorizing. Indeed Francis Bacon's immense width of spiritual vision has been sadly overlooked and misunderstood. It calls for a new understanding in our time of awakening.

Scientific thinking opened the door to our great technology and a true exploration of the nature of substance. But it meant that, in one gesture of thought, we cut out the possibility of grasping the reality of the super-sensible worlds, the invisible realms of being and spirit. It meant that man deliberately cut himself off from becoming what Blake called "the vast being of the Imagination". In order to investigate Nature through the senses, he had to become a mere observer, limiting himself into the equivalent of a one-eyed, colour-blind pointer-reader. He explored Nature by measuring her, rather than apprehending the vision of wholeness which could unite with the vast living Oneness of Divine Being.

The result was a great technology and a so-called 'conquering of Nature' , but in the process man has lost himself as a spiritual being. He has become a mere onlooker. Our task now is to overcome the onlooker-consciousness and discover again that as a divine experiment, humanity is integrally one with the whole and therefore capable of blending consciousness with the divine intelligence.

The development of experimental science and rational materialism was by no means a mistake. Obviously it can bring immense advantage to humanity. We may even see that it was the destiny of western man to take the intellectual plunge into matter and reveal the wonders of creation. For, as the Greeks knew, knowledge begins with wonder. But the price of our achievement has been great. We have had to cut out the realms of spirit, for our necessary decision had been to believe nothing which we could not prove with the senses. The five main senses are attuned to the slow, heavy vibratory rate of matter and therefore cannot apprehend the high frequencies of the invisible, spiritual worlds. Therefore these worlds simply disappeared for us. No longer could we see the elemental realm of the nature spirits or communicate with the angelic kingdom. God Himself was thrown into doubt.

The explanation of this change is simple enough. We know now that the analyzing, intellectual, masculine faculties are associated with the left hemisphere of the brain and this has enabled us to develop a great technology. But in the process we have allowed the faculties of the right hemisphere to go dormant and atrophy. These are the more sensitive, feminine, artistic faculties which can apprehend the living oneness and, through imaginative vision, know the reality of spirit and of God.

Now humanity stands at the threshold when it becomes possible for the scientific mind to take the step into exploration of the super-sensible worlds. Our scientific investigation has revealed that the solidity of matter is an illusion and that all is energy in perpetual flow and movement. Thus we recover the knowledge that all nature, in its apparent diversity, is a great living Oneness, of which humanity is integrally part. Our rational materialism had resulted in the world-view that saw the human being as an accident of chance natural selection in an essentially non-living universe. Therefore he felt himself justified in exploiting nature and the resources of the planet to his own advantage and profit. The results are now obvious, and we see that we bid fair to destroy the whole web of life on Earth.

Now in our generation comes the great turn-about in consciousness. We recover the vision which the Ancient Wisdom of the mystery temples always knew—that the universe is Mind, a vast continuum of living thought, an ocean of life and intelligence. The Earth is then seen as a living, integral being of which mankind is destined to become the brain and nervous system. So far from being mere on-lookers, we, as the crown of Nature, are the rightful stewards of the planet, but we have failed lamentably and culpably in our stewardship.

Now it becomes possible to take a leap in consciousness, re-awaken the faculties of imaginative perception and blend thinking again with the great Oneness of universal Mind.

Surely one of the most remarkable phenomena is the existence of certain individuals who, in all epochs, have made the breakthrough into 'all knowledge'. The mystics and 'illuminati', initiated into higher wisdom, demonstrate that the human potential is virtually unlimited. Such a shift into expanded consciousness was almost inexplicable to our earlier psychology. Now the merging of the streams of scientific and spiritual knowledge makes it clear that humanity stands on the threshold of a breakthrough into direct knowledge of the super-sensible and spiritual worlds. The "peak experience", as Maslow called it, is the counterpart of the initiation which was given in the mystery temples to selected candidates prepared to undergo the necessary ordeals. In Egyptian and Greek days, the general public were taught by means of myth and legend and the drama which arose out of them. We see that the great myths of mankind enshrine the truth about man's spiritual nature. They tell the one great story in infinite variety of forms—the tale that the human soul is an immortal, imperishable droplet of Divinity descending from the realms of Light into the darkness of the material world and sojourning there for a spell, until it finds its higher self, is united in true love and so led back again to the eternal plane from which it descended. The deep fascination of the myths is that they speak directly to the deeper levels of our nature and to the subconscious, and give the profound assurance that we are each, in essence, deathless and immortal sparks of Divinity on the long evolutionary journey into higher consciousness.

The peak experience brings direct, 'noetic' knowledge of the truth and reality of the spiritual worlds. All who have had this experience know that such certainty is possible. They have been initiated. Every one of the great religions has in its origin been grounded in esoteric wisdom, teaching the path which can open the soul to direct knowledge and the sense of the presence of God. In each path, however different it may appear, the goal is the same—a knowledge and experience of the great oneness of all life in God. The emergence of the holistic world-view is in line with all the esoteric paths to knowledge. Inevitably as every religion spread, it was necessary for its priesthood to develop exoteric forms which all could accept. The tragedy has been that the original esoteric wisdom was too frequently treated as heresy to be suppressed. Thus mankind's Golden Rule has been largely ignored. It is laid down by every religion in almost identical words.

Do nothing to others that you would not have them do to you.

This maxim holds the essence of wisdom.

What then is the significance of the mystical experience of the initiate, that intensification of consciousness and blending of mind with the Divine Mind? It is genuine illumination, an almost indescribable state of glory, happiness and love, coupled with direct experience of an all-pervading consciousness, an omnipresent Cosmic being. It is the goal of human evolution, an amazing psychological transformation that brings a sense of unity into the multiplicity of the universe. Human faculties extend to unite with the universal Intelligence, thus completely transcending the 'onlooker consciousness'. A life energy, imperceptible to the lower senses, is experienced. This universal energy, known as *prana*, lies behind the amazing organisation and instincts of all living creatures.

The whole ocean of prana appears to be in a state of flux, flowing towards us and lifting mankind. There comes to the mystic an experience of Light—the activity of a luminous form of thought-energy, which bathes everything in its lustre. This enchanting light is alive. It pulsates with life and intelligence. There is one unbounded ocean of cosmic Intelligence, one almighty actor, known to Hinduism as *Brahma*. Consciousness is the bedrock of all creation, the dominant reality. All visible things are seen as images projected by an all-embracing consciousness.

It must appear that the average brain is now ripe for the manifestation of a mode of cognition superior to the sense-bound thinking. Sense-free thinking is able to perceive and experience the ocean of cosmic Intelligence existing in the boundless universe.

We come to see that an all-knowing Intelligence controls the destiny of humanity. Every human being is a ray of the divine Light. The unification of mankind will only come through wide dissemination of knowledge of the glory dwelling in every human being.

Illumination is the culminating point of evolution, the goal to compensate for all suffering and effort. Evolutionary forces are working to lift personality to higher states of cognition, remodelling the delicate tissues of the brain and balancing its two hemispheres. Then can come an evolutionary leap, a prelude to the birth of a superior race. Our Earth is the seedbed for something new in the universe—the emergence of a part of creation which itself becomes consciously creative.

The inspiration and revelation to which mystics and geniuses have access represent the re-emergence of ideas and concepts already present in another dimension. The soul perceives its glory as a deathless ray of an infinitely intelligent, almighty spiritual Sun. We live indeed in a multi-dimensional universe. What the senses can perceive is but one solitary and limited dimension. Super-sensible perception is now developing and the all-seeing eye of the mind can be opened. A leap in evolution of mind can disclose other planes of creation completely hidden from the rational intellect.

The illuminati or talented ones are the spearhead of humanity and in them the streams of science and mysticism meet. The stage is surely set for the next leap in the advancement of learning, to bring scientific awareness of the wonder of the Universe.

We discover that Mind itself is the architect of creation. It permeates all atoms and molecules as life permeates cells and tissues. The mystical experience provides evidence of an almighty Intelligence hidden behind the cosmos. Throughout all ages the clairvoyants, occultists, sensitives and psychics reveal phenomena that transcend our rational concepts about matter and its laws.

Transcended consciousness opens to us as the goal of evolution which is headed towards a transhuman state. The birth of a unified planetary mind, aware of its essential divinity, is what Teilhard de Chardin called "noo-genesis", the homing upon the Omega point. We recognise an evolutionary thrust towards higher consciousness for humanity, unlocking spiritual potential hitherto dormant. This is the path of enlightenment, for the advancement of the human race to a higher state.

Veritably a new human species is emerging to which the scientist John White gave the name Muller/Homo Sapiens Noeticus. This implies a human being, male/female in balance, of developing consciousness. Conscious constructive control and direction of the self is the goal, for this is the one point in the Universe for which we are each responsible. The holistic world-view teaches us that humanity is indeed one organism of which we are each a cell. Therefore if we hurt others we are hurting ourselves, since the law of karma holds good everywhere. Thus out of the holistic vision a new human being emerges and a new society based not on competition and getting for self by violence, but on caring, co-operation and love for all life. Here are "the meek that shall inherit the earth", for behind them is all the power of the Universe, which now appears to be releasing a forcefield of light and love for the cleansing of the planet. This is the real meaning of the Parousia, the coming of the Cosmic Christ, Avatar of Love, flooding heart and mind.

I close with a few lines from a poem by Evelyn Nolt called:

> ### THE GLORY WHICH IS EARTH
>
> *Man tread softly on the Earth.*
> *What looks like dust*
> *is also stuff of which galaxies are made.*
>
> *The green of Earth's great trees and simple grasses*
> *is the same music played in red*
> *Throughout our trunks and limbs.*
>
> *O Earth, living, breathing, thinking Earth,*
> *On the day we treasure you*
> *As you have treasured us*
> *Humanness is born.*
>
> *And throughout all Light*
> *A Radiance leaps from star to star*
> *Singing: A Son in born*
> *H U M A N I T Y.*

Ocean of Intelligence

So WE COME to the Ocean of Intelligence, of Cosmic Thought. "Without beginning the Law creates life and thought." From the God source pours forth living Thinking, creative Power, the archetypal ideas of all things. There can be no things that are not first concepts in the Divine Mind. So we grasp the conception of the vast sea of intelligence, which in fact is the field of action of angelic beings who are strands of the mind of God. First comes the archetype, the thought being which then manifests in form and substance.

We men are created in this way. Our sensitive body could not be unless it was first thought—by God. Obviously the simpler creatures 'do their thing' by instinct, without conscious understanding. But here in the material plane is this strange and beautiful creature who can also think. It has a brain and consciousness. But thinking isn't brought about by the brain. On the contrary, brain, that fabulous organ, is created by thought in order to reflect the world of Thought.

We can easily see that the eye does not create light. It is an organ which can reflect light and see colour. Because it is sunlike it can see the sun. The ear in its complexity is made by sound to reflect sound. So the brain is an organ of perception which can reflect the thinking that made it. The thought of God creates. The thinking of man reflects Ideas. We are peripheral in a vast process. But we have the unique capacity of being able to think about our thinking. Eye can't see itself. Ear can't hear itself, but thinking can think itself. We can think about our thinking. We can watch that point where ideas emerge, like a spring bubbling fresh water. At this point we are at one and the same time both observer and creator.

To our perception the world appears to be composed of innumerable separate things. Our senses initially give us the illusion of apartness. They can merely reflect the form of things, but not the meaning. Meaning comes when thinking grasps the Idea, the concept within the thing. The concept tree, or oak tree, arises in my mind as I approach the object in the wood. Grasp that this idea of tree *is* in fact integrally part of the tree. The idea is the archetype of God-thought which has been realized (made real) in material form. And when it is approached by thinking man, that idea lights up in his consciousness. Idea is integrally part of tree. Thinking finds relationship between things. We arrive at the realization that the realm of Ideas, the creative thoughts, the archetypes, is a vast Oneness of relationship, a self-sustaining ocean of intelligence. And we each stand separated and peripheral, first feeling ourselves to be isolated entities, over against things, in apartness. Then we see that man in unique in that he also has a *sense of thought*.

This subtler sense enables him to apprehend the idea which is part of every thing. Thus every object could be the gateway of entry into the integrated sea of thinking. The idea of a thing is for every human being the same idea. We may each interpret it according to our make-up and understanding, but what we must strive to grasp is that the ocean of intelligence containing all the Ideas of all things, is a living, self-sustaining organism. If we can learn to watch our thinking at the point where the inner fountain bubbles up, we have the point of entry into knowledge. As we apprehend the Idea, objects cease to be mere separated things but take on meaning and relationship.

Living Ideas

THE COSMIC CHRIST has descended to Earth and taken over the whole field of the etheric forces working in nature. He IS the Life. This He has said again and again. "I AM the resurrection and the Life." "I AM the life within every form of Nature and therefore also in your own heart and if you can raise the thinking of the heart you will find ME." Michael, the countenance of the Christ, is also known as Lord of the Cosmic Intelligence.

Conceive the great ocean of Intelligence poured out of the divine Source. It is alive. It is composed of living ideas, strands of God thought, living energies of thinking, which are self-actuating, selective and able to take on form and metamorphose themselves. These are indeed the angels, and the name given by Moses when he explored this realm, implies energy imbued with the quality of divine Life. These living ideas can in a sense incarnate through entering human thinking and are thus released to operate on the Earth plane. But think what it means that this realm of flowing, weaving, archetypal thinking and intelligence has been allowed by its lord, Michael, to fall down to Earth and therefore become available to humanity. Our intellectual thinking is naturally bound to the senses and the brain. The intellectual left-hemisphere of the brain has even conceived that thoughts are somehow secreted by the brain. But holistic vision brings the conviction that all material forms, the physical brain included, are made by spirit. The convolutions of the brain reflect the convolutions of the flowing ocean of the Cosmic Intelligence.

We may see the brain as a wondrous organ for reflecting ideas. Man, the Divine droplet, imprisoned in the cage of the senses, is, in his poised head, open like a chalice to the heavenly thoughts. Spiritual beings could live in our thinking. Our minds can bear higher beings, who are the angelic strands of the Divine ocean of mind. But this realm is not open to us until we have lifted out of the low vibration of sense-bound thinking. We have to raise ourselves up the Jacob's Ladder of the frequencies, so that we can receive the higher vibration of the Cosmic Intelligence.

Now see that this can operate only in the immediate NOW, that intersection point of the timeless with time. But NOW is perpetually moving on to the next moment. Here is our clue. In the immediate NOW we are in touch with our Higher Self as the gateway to the Cosmic Intelligence. If we can, moment to moment, remain attuned, then the flow of living ideas could continue. This implies that we could within our thinking listen to thoughts which are totally new to us.

Struggle now to see this point. There is a bubbling spring within the mind.

> *O for the wonder that bubbles into my soul.*
> *I would be a good fountain, a good well head,*
> *Would blur no whisper, spoil no expression.*
>
> (D.H. Lawrence)

How do we explore into God? We are very near to the clue now. Realize that the point at which ideas bubble in is, for you, unique in the universe, for it is the one point where you are both creator and at the same time observer of a process. Palpably you are creator. *You* think the thoughts and are responsible. This delicate arrangement leaves you perfect freedom, for you have no obligation to follow them, since you thought them. But also you are watching creation going on. The creative source thinks and speaks through you. It has been well said that "Genius is the most effective channel for the creative source". (*Sir Donald Tovey*) The human being, housed in the body temple, is the perfect channel for the Heaven world of living idea to pour creatively into the material plane. We can tap the ocean of Cosmic Intelligence. Remember what Paul said:

I live, yet not I but Christ lives in me.

We touch the moment of human potential. But there is a warning note. Don't be tempted to say: "It's not me who wrote that poem or spoke those inspired words. They just came through me." We are responsible for every expression, since we are free beings. Yet, at the same time, we are privileged to be conscious channels of divine thought and creative action, and must learn our craft if we are to be an effective channel for the Word.

In the NOW we could think and speak thoughts and ideas which we absolutely had never known before. This suggests a power quite different from academic intellectual thinking, which grows out of the onlooker consciousness. The really inspired lecturers are not merely those who, like a kind of medium, surrender consciousness and allow some higher being to speak through them (which may be perfectly valid and very illuminating), but those who can listen to the bubbling spring and on the instant turn it into human thoughts and verbal expression. Then a lecture could become a genuine exploration into higher realms. "The enterprise is exploration into God." Jesus himself said to his disciples "Do not think beforehand what you are going to say, for in that same hour I shall put the words into your mind".

We know that we approach a period when social structures may crumble and reform and even earth changes may come upon us, but we are urged to have no fear. If we can now learn to remain attuned to the Higher Self in the ever fleeting NOW, we may move securely through times of crisis and change.

We touch here the clue to creative action. It is only in this NOW that the Higher Self can operate. One way it works is to speak in that impulse in the heart suggesting a new course of action in response to a critical situation. But then all too often the cold intellect blocks it off and diverts us.

The higher world of the Michaelic beings working in the Cosmic Intelligence is there to transmute ideas into creative action. But normally we revert to known habit patterns or grooves of thought already experienced and these may have no relevance to totally new situations. The image comes of a tiger let loose in Piccadilly at rush hour. Its glorious instincts are now useless and it will be bewildered. How do we move through totally new conditions with poise and control? We have to learn to act into our Higher Self, on courses suggested by that flash in the heart. Really *act*: but you are called on to act a part which you cannot con beforehand. It is exciting. We must learn to rely on intuitive guidance in the moment, as we would have to do if escaping from a prison camp. Surely it becomes a kind of dance with destiny. Not reliance on chance, but a working with a higher intelligence in the creative instant. Then we can break new ground. Humankind can now cross the threshold and think totally new thoughts, express them in new ways, and act creatively in co-operation with the integral world of the Higher Selves.

Redemption Through
the Power of Love

THINK NOW INTO the vision of Wholeness.

Use imagination to conceive the Universe as a great Mind, an ocean of Divine life and thought.

See that humanity is an organ of consciousness of the living Earth. The planet Earth is a living creature, of which we humans are integrally part. We are that point in Nature where the planet becomes self-conscious.

It is an illusion that we are all separate. We are no more separate than are the cells of the body. Humanity is a single organism of consciousness. Through our eyes the angels can look out at the wonder of the work of creation.

We comprehend that the Universe is Mind, that everything is living Spirit poured out of the Mind of God. First comes the ocean of living ideas, which we call the angelic hierarchies. The angels are strands of the thought of God, cosmic energy, so alive that they can embody themselves on any planetary level. The body is the temple into which a spiritual being, a droplet of Divinity can descend to Earth.

Our sense-bound intellect has difficulty in really comprehending the Oneness vision of the spiritual nature of man and the universe. The imagination and intuition can lift clear of the sense world and gravity, and enter the buoyant, expansive realm of ethereal space, which we may call levity. There is indeed a force which is the polar opposite to gravity.

In consciousness we can float free of gravity and fall upwards towards the great circumference. We recover the thought of levity, the pole of lightness, life, expansion, joy and love, the realm of creative idea and Spirit, which is the opposite to gravity, the grave, the death pole, the weight and darkness of matter.

Truly the human being is a creature perfectly balancing gravity and levity. So also is the tree. With the inner eye we can 'see' the working of levity in plant and tree. When the plant is uprooted it withers until you replant it and water it, so that the energy of life can begin to flow again. We human beings are truly rooted in the spiritual world. Through our materialistic thinking we have become an uprooted species and therefore are dying. It is urgent that we replant ourselves in the spirit. Then again the divine energies can flow through us and we shall come alive.

We are spiritual beings imprisoned in sense and matter and caught in the time scale of past and future. We are bedevilled by a sense of guilt and remorse about the past and fear of the future. This is just what the forces of darkness want—to capture the human soul and bind it to the temporal.

Today, this instant NOW, is the moment when God is ever present. In the *now* we can be continually in touch with our Higher Self and our angelic guides. Here is the clue to living courageously through an age of change. We are imprisoned, but we have discovered that the door is unlocked. All we have to do is to push it and walk out, but this needs courage, for then we step into a new world. But in this ever-moving *Now* moment, the divine energy can flow and our Higher Self can guide us into courses of action we have never conceived before. It is like dancing with destiny, moment to moment, into the creative new.

Let that which is outdated crumble and fall away so that a New Age can come to birth. Accept change with joy. The greatest saga in human history is being played out. The great drama reaches its final act and we all have a part to play.

There never was such a generation in which to be alive. We

are truly children of God. The great message is "Change your thinking, for the realm of spirit is within you". Take the conscious step to realise that the Kingdom, the realm of living spirit is here now, everywhere and within the secret chamber of your heart. If we remain attuned to our Higher Self and our angel guide, we are surrounded by a force-field of light and love which gives absolute protection. In the immediate moment *now*, the intuition can receive the divine information needed for us to act into the unknown, attuned to the living Wholeness.

After aeons of slow evolution, we have come to that dramatic point when we can step clear of the bondage to matter, sense and gravity. If we can consciously channel the thought and power of the divine world, then the human potential is absolutely unlimited. Really a new human species is coming to birth.

Humanity has been given the divine gift of freedom, to become heirs of God. In our world crisis humanity in its ignorance, greed and egoism, has forgotten God and bids fair to destroy the entire web of life on this beautiful planet. But such destruction cannot be allowed, for the whole solar system is also a living organism. The spiritual Sun is the heart centre and the planets compare with the endocrine glands in our body. When one of these goes sick, the whole body is diseased. Earth has gone dark and ill, and humanity, that living organism, has gone cancerous through deviating from the Divine Law. Therefore a cleansing operation has been launched by the Divine world. That which is evil must be cauterized or washed away.

The darkness of our dramatic time may prove to be an image of the cleansing. The great truth is that a spiritual force-field of Light and Love is being flooded into the world of matter, raising the frequency rate to a high solar vibration. It is the nature of any magnetic field that it repels what is not capable of vibrating with it. This force-field is living energy, and it will draw all those human particles which can attune to it, and reject and repel those who, of free choice, continue on the path of violence, hate and cruelty, blood-shed and fear. Thus a new world is coming about. A redemptive power pours through the invisible force-field, harmonizing all life. This power must be called Love. It is God in action. To the negative dark forces, it will seem like the angel of Death riding the dark horse. It is a force which overwhelms the darkness. The human soul is immortal. For it there can be no death, so those who will not yet turn to God will be shepherded on to some other planetary level, while the cleansing operation is completed and a new age brought to birth.

Here is what Teilhard de Chardin called "the wild hope that *our* earth is to be recast". The world is so mad and bad and wicked, that if rational materialism were the only truth, we might as well give up. Let us eat, drink and be merry, for tomorrow we die—by the million! But it is not the truth. Materialism is hopelessly inadequate to explain the fantastic mystery of the living universe. And just because the alternative is now so grim, it is surely valid to grasp and hold this marvellous conception that God is now in action, present everywhere and personified for our understanding in our own time.

This is not to say that we can sit back and leave it all to God. Out of the wholeness of the living Universe pours the redemptive power of love, which can sweep away and transform all that vibrates on a lower and coarser level. Darkness fights the light, but cannot win that battle. We all have a part to play in this drama, since, given freedom, we must take the initiative to attune and call upon the angelic world.

The coming of the New Age is not someone's thought-out plan. It is a phenomenon of metamorphosis, the raising of the vibratory rate in matter through this force-field of light, love and power, and we are the channels through whom this force can flow. Let us give ourselves over to this great and glorious event and welcome it.

We are privileged to be among the forerunners who can pave the way for the coming of God. The long, tragic and gallant history of humanity now reaches a point of consummation, when God can enter consciousness. He is always everywhere, for he IS Life and Love. But we must now lift consciousness so that humanity can be reborn. This planet of ours is giving birth to something new in the Universe, a seed of creation, a new species bound by love to the conscious creative service of God. Let us rejoice. For this we exist. To take this step, to channel the redemptive power of Love, is all that matters now. Then a New Age will truly be born.

Potentials for a New Renaissance

CONCEIVE that each one of us is a spiritual being on an infinitely long path of experience. The being within us that can say 'I Am' is, in fact, an immortal, spiritual droplet of Divinity, housed for the time being in the temple of a body. Think that. It is not dogma to be believed.

You can't *prove* it with the rational, logical intellect. We are concerned with learning how to explore into spiritual ideas with our thinking. The first and basic idea is that we are each of us a spark of the Divine fire, a droplet of the Divine ocean, and as such are axiomatically immortal and imperishable. We always were and we always will be.

In order to explore and experience the fascinating world of matter, we have entered into this divinely designed temple of the body. This means that in the deep cellular memory and soul, consciousness goes right back to the beginning in Eden Garden. This understanding can come as soon as we accept the doctrine of re-incarnation as the only possible explanation of life on Earth. Now we see the potentiality of a new Renaissance. Will you in this light look back into the great Renaissance of 15th century Italy? We all passed through that phase of evolution. Consciousness is always evolving and the sweep of human consciousness is best indicated in Blake's trilogy: From *Innocence* through *Experience* and on to *Imagination*. In the primal innocence of Eden, we were in the pre-Fall conditions, when the entity in each of us was identified with the great Oneness of the total divine Being of humanity.

Then we experienced the Fall, gradually descending into matter, to become embedded in physical form and the sense world. Now look back. The memory is within you. Look right back in imagination to the Garden.

> *Very old are we men. Our dreams are tales*
> *Told in dim Eden by Eve's nightingales.*
>
> (Walter de la Mare)

Conceive the gradual fall, the eternal entity in you getting deeper and deeper into the physical body and the sense world through innumerable earth-lives. Originally our consciousness would be identified with the great oneness of creation, in direct touch with the spiritual and angelic worlds. Then a point when that entity which is You takes the plunge, fully to identify with the physical body and the senses. That is what took place at the beginning of the 15th century in Italy. What happened in the Renaissance is the outward symptom of this deep spiritual and psychological change, when the ego of man takes the step of complete identification with the physical body and the senses. (Let me make it quite clear that whenever we use the word MAN, it refers genetically to species male/female: And God said: "Let us make Man after our own Image. Male and female created He them.") This would mean we were suddenly aware of the beauty of the body and the excitement of the world of nature around us. Delighting in a new form of exploration and experimentation, we would have lost the experience of ourselves as a spiritual being.

When you consider what happened in the Renaissance, this makes sense. There was an immense release of creative energy through the human entity really taking over embodiment and beginning to explore the glory and excitement of the sense world. There was also a violent manifestation of egoism. The sensitives and initiates must have felt that something grave was happening. Humanity was taking a plunge into the seductions and excitement of the material plane and this would imply a loss of contact with the world of living ideas and Spirit. Man is bound to lose himself as a spiritual being while finding himself as an ego, controlling Nature. So while the Renaissance released marvellous creativity, it also manifested in violent egoism.

Marlowe's great dramatic trilogy expresses this ego drive.

"The Jew of Malta"—Power through gold.
"Tamberlaine the Great"—Power through conquest.
"Dr Faustus"—Power through knowledge and magic.

We plunge for some centuries deep into matter, but the cycle begins to lead up again, not back to the innocence of Eden, but on to what Blake called *Imagination*, a recovery of the vision of wholeness and the realization that we need not identify only with our separated self as a sense-bound, body-bound creature. We can identify once more with the world of living being, and the unitary nature of humanity as a vast Being of which we are each a tiny cell.

It is interesting that the arts in the Renaissance, particularly painting, are so often a superb expression of man's religious and spiritual nature. It is as if the arts chose to re-affirm that the man is at core a spiritual being, urging us to remember our real identity, as if to say: "You are going for some centuries to plunge into matter and explore it, but you will for the time lose touch with your spiritual source." So in this plunge into materialism and egoism, the Arts give a picture of man's spiritual nature in a universe spiritual in essence.

We have come to conceive that we are each a separated being who has evolved by natural selection and mere chance. Now the great turn-about is taking place in the very centre of human consciousness, a re-discovery of the holistic world-view and a re-awakening to the truth that man is a spiritual being in a universe spiritual in its nature and origin.

By re-identifying with the unitary nature of humanity and by re-attuning in consciousness to the spiritual world, we begin to touch once more the realm of creative ideas and the creative archetypes. If the expression in the Renaissance was so glorious at a time when we were losing touch with the world of spirit, what is going to happen when, in full consciousness, we are received back again into touch with the Divine world? One can foresee that in all the arts there will be an expression such as we cannot yet conceive. It is possible that there may be a new Renaissance, out-shining the great creations of the 15th and 16th centuries.

There could be an inflooding of spiritual power and light, uniting our thinking with the ocean of Thought in the Universe. This is the transformation that could, and will, follow the coming cleansing of the planet. Deep within each of us lies the memory of the long descent from the Garden into experience of the material world and sense-bound thinking. This is the long education of the human race, through many lives in the school of Earth. We are now at the turning point. The time of fulfillment is upon us.

Now, one thing we are realizing is that the human being is *not* an accident of chance natural selection, a mere observer over against nature. We *are* Nature. We are that point where nature becomes self-conscious. As Alexander Pope put it:

> *Mere atoms, casually together hurled*
> *could ne'er produce so beautiful a world.*

We may see Nature as a wondrous work of art and design, and we are central to it. Our imagination may grasp that there is a drive within the whole of nature for the formation of the human being as a point of self-consciousness which can, of free choice, come back to the Father as a friend of God and co-creator. Such is the divine purpose of life on Earth.

Grasp the conception that the Whole is an amazing design and is watched over and superintended. There is a 'super-intention' behind the whole of evolution—to create on this gem of a planet a setting in which self-consciousness can come about, in a being carrying a nervous system and brain and a capacity for emotion. Nature thus becomes conscious of itself, but we are still a part of the Great Whole, the ocean of Divine thought. Out of the creative Source pours the ocean of Life and Thought, ideas in the Mind of God.

First in creation God thinks the archetype of Man like unto Himself, a being, male-female in nature, who can focalize thought, love and creative will. We are deceived if we think that because man is last to appear in creation he must have evolved out of the primates. No! He is first in creation, though last to appear in physical form, when the complex setting of the natural world has been prepared for him. Now cast your mind forward through many aeons and many lives—for the whole of eternity is yours.

We are working towards the realizing of the great human idea. What shall we be as artists, as athletes, as lovers, thinkers and enjoyers and creators, when at last we fully realize the archetype? In Jesus, in the Buddha, and in figures like Leonardo and Michelangelo, the potential has been revealed in embodiment. We are all moving towards this potential. The implication is that we now stand on the threshold of a birth and awakening. In a deeper sense humanity is *not yet born*. We stand at the point for which the universe has been preparing us through the incredibly beautiful creation of the body, as the temple to receive the descent of soul and spirit into the material plane.

Does it not imply that there is a drive within the universe to attain self-consciousness? Our beautiful planet is truly the seed point from which something new in the universe is being born. We stand at the threshold when man can become truly human and in freedom become a friend of God, a co-creator. No wonder it appears that the higher worlds are deeply interested in this planet as aeons of evolution culminate at the opening of the Aquarian Age. The forces of darkness strive to drag us down and negate the great Divine experiment of human freedom. But the light and love and power of the Christ must win, even though a cleansing of the planet will be inevitable. If we will in freedom work with the inflooding of this divine power, we may expect a burst of new creativity as the archetype comes to manifestation through us.

We stand therefore on the threshold of a new Renaissance of humanity working directly with the Divine in full consciousness and freedom. We are now fully responsible as to whether we plunge into disaster or work with the inflooding of love and light to transform our world. And we may be certain of the ultimate defeat of darkness by the coming light.

A channelled message from *The Book of Myrddin*:

> *The Earth herself is about to undergo the latest of a number of initiations. Much has been spoken of these coming changes, which, from our perspective, can only be seen as a cleansing, and can only lead to a more enlightened age. Are you ready for these changes?*

And a communication channelled by Paul Solomon:

> *Know that the time is short. The vibrations of this earth are being raised to such a high level, that those not in tune with God's purposes, with His import, with His message, cannot remain on that portion of the Earth that would be so perfected.*

The Human Saga

W E ARE GRASPING the supreme hope that lies within darkest despair, the pearl of great price to be found and won by those that seek. In our extraordinary age, at the close of the 20th century, we very clearly approach a culmination point. Things simply cannot go on as they are without terrible disaster. A technocratic civilization gone mad in the quest for power and profit, overshadowed by terrible fear, rushes headlong towards the abyss. This is a great drama—perhaps the greatest ever staged. We have to learn who are the chief actors, who the producer. Who directs it all? Is it merely blind, inhuman, brutal forces of death? It is a playing-out of the myth of the human soul, and every one of us has a part to play. Indeed like Frodo and Sam, the ringbearers in Tolkein, it must appear that we, little people, do have a very important part to play among the Great Ones who act the leading roles. And in this drama the outcome remains unknown. We all play a part we cannot learn beforehand, for the story unfolds as we enact it.

But what seems increasingly certain is that we as a human race are not merely facing dead forces of destruction, but that behind it all, overshadowing, overlighting, appears to be a vast Intelligence which knows what It is doing and ultimately is Love.

We have gone through the centuries and epochs in which mankind plunged into materialism and lost God in the process. Now into human thinking re-emerges the vision of the sacred, the deep certainty that the Universe is mind and that behind the wisdom poured into all the diverse forms of nature is a great oneness of intelligence. And transfusing this intelligence is an endless ocean working for the harmonizing of all life in a creative on-going flow of true evolution. This is Love and it is alive, permeating everything. Each one of us is a point of consciousness in a sea of greater consciousness.

> *I am a point of Light*
> *Within a greater Light,*
> *I am a strand of loving energy*
> *Within a stream of Love Divine,*
> *I am a spark of sacrificial fire*
> *Focused within the fiery will of God*
> *And thus I stand.*
>
> (via Alice Bailey)

Affairs are now soul-size indeed! Our rational thinking too easily misses the major factor in the world situation and totally ignores its chief allies.

Our generation—*us now*—face the clear possibility of extinction and the complete breakdown of civilization. The world is appalling, mad and wicked, a patriarchal, technocratic culture which has gone insane in its drive for power and profit and is haunted by a terrible fear. It seems that the one real measure of good is whether a thing pays! To the rational, logical mind the future looks grim indeed. That greatest of rationalists, Bertrand Russell, once wrote: "Only on the firm foundation of unyielding despair can the soul's habitation henceforth be safely built."

And yet . . . and yet . . . There is that in the human heart which, blessedly, refuses to despair. In the "Gospel of the Essenes", a variant of the Book of Revelation, John, shown the terrible scenes of suffering and death which face humanity, asked his guide "Then is there no hope, Bright Angel?" "*There is always hope*, O thou for whom heaven and earth were created."

Now note this strange and very significant fact. Though it

seems to the logical mind that irrevocable disaster looms ahead, yet most of the seers, mystics and initiates who have touched the higher vision do *not* see an end of civilization. Change— yes; cleansing of the planet—yes; but total destruction by flood or ice or nuclear bombs; no. They can see ahead through the dark tunnel into the light. Humanity indeed must learn its lesson. That which is evil must be washed away and burned out or cauterized. It cannot be allowed to go on, and the field must be cleansed for a New Age to emerge. We approach the midnight hour. *So* bad is the picture that it is totally valid to hold on to the thread of the supreme hope implicit in the holistic vision now flooding our consciousness. Alan Watts wrote:

> There is so much tragedy on the surface of life that, were there not somewhere, right in the centre of things and in the centre of each and every pain, a state of absolute and unconfined joy accessible to all, the whole realm of Being must be damned. The joyous centre is there and the heart of God is open, in the very midst of every experience that can befall us.

If we can really take and grasp the depth of the holistic world-picture, we must come to feel that there cannot be final extinction by ice, flood or nuclear holocaust. There may be much destruction, earth changes, and local wars, but not the general destruction of a planet. This cannot be tolerated by the high intelligencies of the solar cosmos. This seems to me implicit in holism and the spiritual world-view. Let us explore it and then see the part we have to play and how we can implement it and train ourselves for our role of 'freedom fighters'—for every man and woman is called upon by free choice to ally with the forces of Light which now are cleansing the planet.

How do we make ourselves worthy of this task?

PART II

*A
Personal
Quest*

Something of Autobiography

Through Agnosticism into Holistic Vision

THE WHOLENESS VISION in our time does challenge us to cross the threshold of consciousness and explore into higher knowledge—into God. We are all called on to attempt this in our own way and all can start now from where we are.

We are seeking the path to spiritual knowledge, to find how we can learn to think spiritual IDEAS. In our time wonderful revelations are being given by those advanced souls who have had what is called the "peak experience", a breakthrough into higher knowledge which brings direct and absolute certainty that the Universe is a great Mind. Those of us who are not in that category can nevertheless set forth on the exploration.

It is to all on this quest that I dedicate this book.

Perhaps it would be helpful if I gave a brief autobiography, to show how this exploration developed in my own case. My family was agnostic, my father an avowed atheist. None of us six children was baptized and we rarely saw the inside of a church—except for my younger sister Katharine, who knew God from childhood. My parents were in that cultural stream devoted to the service of mankind but without religious belief or any expectation of survival after death. My family tradition was one of liberal and radical politics. My uncle was the great historian, G.M. Trevelyan, my grandfather Sir George Otto Trevelyan was one of Gladstone's cabinet and author of a fine history of the American Revolution, my father, a liberal M.P., who during the first World War came over to Labour and was Minister of Education under Ramsay MacDonald in 1924 and 1928 in the first Labour governments. They were great orators.

As a young man at Cambridge I thought that I too wanted to go in for politics, but my path was to be very different.

Up to the age of thirty-six, I had no concern with the Spirit and no religious belief. Then came the turning point, in 1942. Let me briefly lead up to that event. I was born in Westminster on 5th November 1906 at 9.25 p.m. Those concerned with astrology will know what it means to have Scorpio as Sun sign with Leo rising. The time puts Leo exactly on the cusp of the 12th House. Thus my life shows these qualities fairly clearly— the reserve and secretiveness of Scorpio and the outgoing and sunny front of Leo, the actor and public speaker.

My life has been marked by a series of enthusiasms which overlaid the darker scorpionic propensities. The first of these was for caves! We were sent during the first war to Sidcot, the Quaker co-education school in the Mendip Hills of Somerset. Here, as an older boy, I found a passion for cave-exploring. A small group of us were given permission to explore on free days in the caverns of Mendip. I lived and dreamed caves and doubtless this great sport, with its adventuring into the mysteries and wonders of the darkness underground, had deep psychological significance! Certainly it was a thrill!

I recall a Christmas gathering with all the family and cousins, in which our Grandmother wrote a little verse about each one of us young people. Mine ran:

> *There was a young person called George*
> *Whom all of his family adorge,*
> *And he loves them too*
> *But between me and you*
> *Not so much as a cave or a gorge.*

This summed me up completely!

In 1925 I went up to Trinity College, Cambridge, to which all my family had been. I, rather inevitably, fell into reading history as the family subject. Here my scorpionic reserve caused me trouble. I was, strangely, never able to discuss my future or my career with anyone. I was innerly somewhat adrift, but threw myself into Cambridge life with enthusiasm. This involved debating, fencing, dancing with the Cambridge Morris Men under Rolf Gardiner, illicit roof climbing with friends from the Cambridge Mountaineering Club. Mountains and climbing came to mean a great deal to me.

One unusual activity should be mentioned. This was the Man Hunt in the great hills of the Lake District, invented by my uncle, G. M. Trevelyan, and the mountaineer Geoffrey Winthrop Young when they were at Trinity in 1898 and running still, always Mastered by one of my family. Some twenty or thirty men gather for the three days of Whitsun at Seatoller in Borrowdale. Three hares are sent out at dawn with red scarves round their shoulders, to be hunted till dusk. It is an absolutely epic sport. I revived it after the war in 1948 and ran it as Master till 1967 when my younger brother Geoffrey took over. The Hunt is well set for its centenary in 1998 with my nephew Robin Dower as Master.

After Cambridge, undecided on a career, I went to Germany for six months in 1928, at the time when Hitler's Brown Shirts were emerging as a force. There I made some contact with the Freischaar, that liberal aspect of the German Youth Movement which could have swung Germany in a very different direction. I had developed a real interest in architecture, discovered the Bauhaus at Dessau, and made a personal link with Gropius and Moholy Nagy, and even, quixotically, signed on to train in the office of a modern architect, Breuhaus.

But this was not to be. Coming back to England to sort things out, a friend, with perception, simply said "What about Crafts?" In a flash I knew that this was what I must do. I had studied the medieval crafts guilds, but as an intellectual it had never occurred to me that one could actually make things oneself. A passionate longing filled me. I soon realised that woodwork and furniture was my line and after a little enquiry found that the fountain head was the workshop of Peter Waals at Chalford in Gloucestershire. The Cotswold furniture tradition was inaugurated by Ernest Gimson and his friends Sidney and Ernest Barnsley, architects personally inspired by William Morris. Peter Waals had been foreman to Gimson and took over the workshops after his death.

It was a wonderful experience for a young man to come into that workshop. My bench in the old mill room was next to that of Ernest Smith, the foreman, who had been with Gimson as an apprentice. There were twelve men working, all trained in this superlative tradition of fine construction, mostly in solid woods. I could watch the making of a cabinet here, a bureau there, a dozen chairs at the next bench, a dining table or a wardrobe. I myself made the chamfered bed which I still sleep in, a tall fall-front bureau at which I now write, my armchair and other pieces. For nearly two years I lived in the bliss of creative activity. It was a great privilege and experience to work as student-apprentice in a large craft workshop and I learned the significance of surrendering oneself totally to the discipline of a great tradition before attempting to design oneself.

The Cotswolds have for me a magic through this experience. The Chalford workshops closed down in 1937 shortly after Waals' death, but I kept Ernest Smith going with designs of my own for the next ten years.

I see the crafts as integrally part of the holistic vision and the alternative life-style that grows out of it. Naturally a craftsman has no need to be concerned with the spiritual world-view. But once we have seen that the Earth is an integral living being, that the forms and materials of Nature are the expression of living divine ideas, and that man is integrally part of the wondrous whole, then a new and deeper significance is given to every craft.

But making furniture was not to be my work. On that same weekend, when I knew with certainty that I must become a craftsman, I also took a great decision which hit me with complete clarity. I would master the teaching of the Alexander

Technique and this would be my life's work. Since I give a later chapter to this, I shall not go into it further now. Suffice to say that while at Cambridge I had gone for lessons to F. M. Alexander and knew with full conviction that he had made a discovery of paramount importance for a new humanity. Here was something to which I could give total devotion. The opportunity now presented itself through his deciding to launch the first training course for teachers in 1931. It was typical of my temperament that I should give up everything to this work. None of my family or friends had the least clue what it was about!

For me, the significance lay in the vision of wholeness. The word holistic had not then come into general use. I had not yet achieved any vision of the spiritual nature of man and the universe. But now, looking back, I can see how this step in my life was an essential preparation for what was to follow. I have no doubt that Alexander's technique and teaching about conscious, constructive direction of the use of the self will take its place as a fundamental feature in the emergence of a new life-style and a new humanity.

A group of eight of us went through the three years training course with Alexander. Then, after teaching it for a while, I had to face the fact that I was getting to a point of social isolation that was for me psychologically untenable. I had put everything into it and now had to admit I could not carry it through. Therefore I was left without a career or qualification in 1936, at the age of thirty.

At this point Kurt Hahn, the great headmaster and founder of Gordonstoun School, came into my life. It was clear that I now had to enter a wider field of human contact, and teaching was the obvious line. So I went to Gordonstoun, teaching history, literature, woodwork and outdoor pursuits. This made a fine and full life.

In 1936 I was fired with a new vision—that of using our great country houses as cultural centres for everyone. At Hahn's suggestion I went out to Denmark and Sweden to make contact with the Folk Highschools. This movement had been launched in the 1840's by Bishop Grundvig, to lift the young Danes out of the slough of despond, after a period of depression following the Napoleonic wars. His plan was to run five-month residential courses for young farmers, not to teach them better farming, but to make them better Danes, so that they went back to their farms inspired, through learning about Danish history and literature and Scandinavian mythology and folklore. He felt that "enlivenment" was as important as "enlightenment". Therefore he decreed the *Doctrine of the Living word.* His teachers were to speak from the heart direct to the hearts of their pupils, without using set notes. They were free to shape their own curriculum on themes they themselves found inspiring. The plan worked, and it did much for modern Denmark. I was clear that the Folk Highschool idea could not be applied directly in Britain, but aspects of Grundvig's teaching were of vital significance.

I saw that for England the ideal tool for a new consciousness would be the short residential course in a country house, to break through into wider interests. I am rather proud to have been thinking along these lines in the 1930's, well before the movement for the Short Term residential colleges came to birth. This followed the war years. Sir Richard Livingstone, Oxford Professor of Education, wrote books such as "Education in a World Adrift", in which he urged the need for a new kind of people's college, a cultural centre for all, and what better venue than country houses, many of which had fallen on difficult days. Somewhat quixotically I had the hope that I might in due time use Wallington, our family home in Northumberland, for such a purpose. But this was not to be.

In 1942, when I was 36, occurred the event which changed the course of my life. I had become interested in compost and organic husbandry and sought out the leading adviser, Derryk Duffy, in Heathcote House, near Aberdeen. I found him busy with a conference of twenty leading members of the Anthroposophical movement, studying Rudolf Steiner's agriculture course. Derryk was a bit bored at having to give time to a visitor, but showed me the garden and the compost heaps. Then, since I had turned up, they suggested that in the evening they should break into the general programme and invite Dr Walter Johannes Stein to give a general lecture entitled "What did Dr Steiner mean by Anthroposophy?"

That hour was a revelation. Stein was an advanced clairvoyant and initiate. I am certain that he knew precisely what he was doing. The lecture was given directly to me, though he never looked at me. All the great concepts of Spiritual Science came up one after the other and my whole soul innerly shouted affirmation to him. "Pre-existence—yes, yes, obviously; Earth as training ground for souls—yes, indeed!; therefore Reincarnation through many lives—obviously yes; Universe as Mind and living thought—Earth as a living creature—yes, yes!" For that whole hour no negative response rose in me. The agnosticism of thirty-six years faded like morning mist. The spiritual world-view was clear to me in its glory and wonder.

I have no doubt that this event in my life was planned and staged by higher destiny and that the timing was ripe for a leap in consciousness. I owe Walter Stein the profoundest debt of gratitude for what he did that night. Thereafter Dr Ernst Lehrs took me over as his pupil, led me into Goethe's thinking about plant metamorphosis and opened the doorway to the understanding of spiritual science. I joined the Anthroposophical Society and read Steiner avidly for the next years. Had I been a bachelor it is likely I would have plunged into Steiner teaching with the same drive as I had entered the field of the Alexander work. But for family reasons it seemed more appropriate to return to Gordonstoun.

My war experience was also in the teaching field. I was commissioned as Captain in the Rifle Brigade, but was posted to the so-called "GHQ Travelling Wings" for training of Home Guard in warfare. Our field was northern Scotland, and I was then appointed as adjutant to the Highland Home-Guard Division based on Inverness.

At the end of the war I went down with jaundice and spent six weeks in an army hospital on a diet of boiled white fish. I came out looking yellow and shrivelled, as if I had been in Belsen. When I recovered and reverted to normal diet, I remember visiting one of the biodynamic gardeners near Nairn and being allowed to sit under a tunnel of green raspberry bushes and pick these delectable fruits and eat them direct and sun-warmed. It was a taste of heaven.

Illnesses often mark karmic turning points in a life. Certainly this seems to with mine. Gordonstoun had kept open my place and I recall walking the six miles from Elgin to take up schoolmastering again. Halfway I found myself going slower and slower, as if some invisible elastic rope was holding me back, or as if some angel barred the way. I can still picture the sandy road with a leaning scots pine. I came to a standstill. There was no conscious reasoning. I just stood and then quietly turned around and walked back to Elgin. I knew that if I once entered Gordonstoun my post-war career would be that of schoolmaster. Now I turned and walked into adult education and an unknown future.

The decision taken, all the enthusiasm for the concept of the cultural centre in the country house came flooding back. I would get into the new movement for the short-term residential colleges. To gain experience I decided to sign on for two years more in the army and take a post of instructor in the No 1 Army College at Dalkeith, which was running two-week courses on every conceivable subject to help men and women from the services to get back into civilian life and qualification. I took a post in the arts department, teaching history and literature, with the hope that in due course I might become a tutor in one of the new colleges now coming to birth.

The dream of using the family home at Wallington proved quite impossible. It would not have been a suitable house, even if I had inherited it as my own. But my father, Sir Charles Trevelyan, decided that after his day Wallington should pass out of private ownership. The estate was not entailed, so he had no obligation to leave it to me as his eldest son. In 1941 he bequeathed the house and the large agricultural estate to the National Trust, the mansion to be maintained from the rent roll of the estate. This set an important precedent for the Trust. By accepting the bequest, they took on the task of becoming landlord and agent to big estates and the lead given at Wallington has been followed in many parts of the country. After my father's death in 1958, the Trust took over and have made Wallington into one of the finest show houses in the North.

For me the door closed on Wallington, but opened on a country house far more suitable for a cultural centre. In 1947 the Shropshire Education Committee advertised for a principal for Attingham Park, the Shropshire Adult College. I applied and against a very strong field was, to my astonishment, appointed. Here was a dream coming true.

Attingham, a noble Georgian mansion built in 1785, was the perfect setting for an adult college. It was the finest of all the group of some twenty-five colleges founded in these years and it was the fourth to come to birth. Lord Berwick, following the lead from Wallington, had bequeathed it to the National Trust. He died just before the opening of the College. Lady Berwick, a gracious presence, lived on in her own apartments. My governing body, tenants of the National Trust, represented many Shropshire interests. Sir Offlay Wakeman, Chairman of the County Council was Chairman of Governors. Birmingham University Department of Extra Mural Studies contributed the salary of a tutor and were closely linked. The instigator of the whole plan, Martin Wilson, the Secretary for Education, was Clerk to the Governors.

This, however, was a quite new venture. No one had experience of a short-term adult college. So, very wisely, they decided that the actual programme planning and direction must be left entirely to the Principal. Attingham was to become a hub of adult educational activity for the county and region. I was given complete freedom in creating the activities, though it was all closely watched. Martin Wilson made some excellent appointments of adult tutors for the county, so with the tutors from the Extra-Mural Department we made a fine team.

Attingham grew into a focal centre for a great number of stimulating activities. I was to be there for twenty-four years till my retirement in 1971. In that period I calculate that we laid on 1,033 open courses on an infinite variety of subjects. Often two courses were run at a weekend with closed conferences midweek.

I made a point of joining in and actually running one of the courses every weekend. This was important. I knew, quite simply, that I could enthuse people on any subject I wanted to know about. Thus in those post-war years we broke into theme after theme and subject after subject and I made it the rule that I always gave at least one lecture, even if it was a subject new to me. This, I think, encouraged people to explore new fields. I saw that it was a question of finding what I then called the "integrating ideas" which would relate the subject to a wider context. That would give encouragement to exploration and then the visiting professor or expert could take us to a deeper understanding. I can see that this was in line with holistic thinking, though we had not yet heard the word.

So our programmes touched literature, history, architecture, archaeology, music (both creative and listening), drama, all the crafts, painting, birdsong, butterflies, geology, heraldry and much more—any subject which could arouse enthusiasm and widen vision. Then we arranged concerts with the famous quartets, special lectures and amateur drama. Through the inspired direction of Eric Salmon, the drama adviser, we offered Twelfth Night, The Winters Tale, School for Scandal and other great plays as arena productions in our music room.

The midweek periods were mostly filled with closed conferences and there were summer schools for a week or ten days. At Attingham I also established a ten-day summer school called Creative Leisure, in which students could explore a number of crafts and get creative experience. Bill Campbell and Jeff Lowe directed this dynamic project for twenty years. Among the activities we developed a school of mosaic and the triumph was a zodiac of twelve panels five and a half feet tall to decorate a circular room in the house. These are still displayed in the Library at Wellington, Shropshire.

I also taught the colourful art of heraldry by getting students to paint shields. By so doing, they mastered the picturesque language of 'blazon' and we decorated our refectory with over one hundred shields.

In 1942 I had married Helen Lindsay-Smith. Now at Attingham, on one of my art courses, she discovered a latent talent for painting, which released a creative drive continuing to this day. She filled our house and the College Dining Room with colourful pictures of flowers and plant forms.

We must recognize that the weekend house-party in country houses has been a major factor in English social history, but of course it was confined to the rich upper classes. Now we were experiencing the metamorphosis of the country house-party for everyone from all walks of life. The groups were welded together by a common enthusiasm to explore some cultural subject, theme or activity. Some three thousand people stayed at Attingham each year and an equal number came to concerts and single events. And we must recall the annual course in musical analysis of a major work, conducted by Mary Firth. The success of Attingham owes much to Mrs Orgill, for ten years domestic bursar, and affectionately known as 'Mrs O'.

It was a full and exciting life. My governors had arranged with the National Trust that the college should use the great dining room with its lovely plaster ceiling as lecture and music room. We also had use of the library. Thus the students had a real experience of living in a country house set in its park land with a nearby river.

In 1952, through the initiative of my art-historian friend, Helen Lowenthal, we founded the Attingham Summer School on the Historic Houses of Britain, for American art and architectural historians, museum experts and preservationists. This offered a week of lectures and tours at Attingham, followed by a two-week tour to different regions. It runs to this day and has forged a remarkable link between our two countries on the basis of enjoyment of visiting country houses and studying their architecture and collections.

I have so deep a debt of gratitude to all who worked at Attingham as colleagues, tutors and visiting lecturers, but space does not allow me to mention all by name. It was a great group enterprise and it released creative energy into adult education. Many people were enriched with an enhanced sense of the deeper meaning of life and the potential of the human being.

After twenty-four years the time for retirement approached, for in 1971 I should be sixty-five. To mark the retirement a farewell celebration was held at the end of August 1971, with some five hundred guests and speeches in a great marquee. There was a great flow of warmth and affection on this occasion. As a diversion after tea, I arranged for a balloon to fly from the lawn. The concept of the Warden of Attingham disappearing into the clouds in a hot air balloon was irresistible!

The previous year I was struck by rheumatoid poli-arthritis. This could have been totally crippling. By the time of my retirement I was wearing calipers on my legs and was in a sorry state, but the arthritis was in no way to be allowed to interfere with the holistic enterprise. Illnesses, as I have said, may well mark turning points in our lives, and the arthritis made retirement from Attingham essential, since I was not prepared to let the college run at anything less than :'s traditional pace and pressure. However, I would not consent to hand myself over to medical treatment with drugs and cortizone and gold injections. Then I found my way to Dr Gordon Latto, one of the leading figures in natural therapy in the country. The secret of nature cure is to stop putting into the blood what causes imbalance, and so allow nature to restore us to health. With raw, live food, herbal remedies, hydrotherapy and other nature-cure treatments, we restored the blood to complete normality on every count and the arthritis steadily receded. Some damage to joints was irreversible, but in four or five years I was free from pain, mobile and full of energy and could walk the hills again.

One of my proudest moments was in a great Wrekin Trust conference on Holistic Healing, during a session of questions to the lecturing panel. I was sitting between Gordon Latto and his surgeon brother Conrad. The question came up—"Would the Lattos tell us about the holistic treatment of arthritis". Both brothers turned to me and said, "George, you answer that question." I can categorically declare that rheumatoid arthritis can be overcome by nature-cure methods. In my case the Alexander teaching was also an essential asset.

Adult Education for Spiritual Knowledge

At Attingham I was free to experiment with any themes for courses that would arouse enthusiasm and vision and sense of meaning to life. I remembered a statement by Whitehead which could well have come from Plato: *Moral Education is impossible without habitual Vision of Greatness.* In an age when so many values were slithering, we needed to do all we could to restore sense of meaning. This seemed to me the real task of adult education. We were not so much concerned with current affairs, sociology and economics. These had been the major themes in the great days of the Workers Educational Association. I recall an occasion when our group of newly appointed wardens or principals to the short-term adult colleges, met to hear a lecture by one of the great figures of the W.E.A. He spoke of the Law of Diminishing Enthusiasm, and we looked at each other, knowing that we in the new movement were working with the Law of Mounting Enthusiasm!

Now our form of the new adult education was open to all classes and was clearly concerned to tap interests which added significance to our lives and gave the lead for development of the self through cultivating new skills and wider capacities. For me personally the spiritual world-view gave sense of meaning to life. Therefore from the first I began to experiment. In the very first programme I included a weekend called "What can be believe?'' in which we touched on spiritual knowledge. I also invited my heroes from the Anthroposophical Movement to come and lecture. Dr Lehrs, Dr Stein and Dr Karl König all came to Attingham, but it became clear that the idiom of anthroposophical lectures was not right for this setting. Warnings came to me that I must not risk criticism from rate-payers about what was happening at Attingham. Obviously I had to find ways of presenting these new ideas in a generally acceptable English idiom. I learned to be very diplomatic and play down these courses. The Extra-Mural Department expressed grave doubts as to whether they were valid for adult education!

Yet the governors had given me full freedom, so I continued my experiments in the fifties. At this time we knew little about a 'New Age Movement'. Yet by the early sixties I found that if I laid on a course on "Frontiers of Reality" or "The Quest for the Grail in our Time" or "Spiritual Awakening", the house was packed. Clearly there was a profound need in the field of adult education for teaching about the deeper meaning of life. The news was getting around that here was a country house running spiritual courses, and people flooded in from all over the country. On one occasion the seventy beds were filled by return of post when our programme was sent out. Though my governors were doubtful about these courses, they at least brought in the funds! And to their credit, they never interfered or came to see what happened. And wonderful things did happen, but I learned to play my cards carefully.

In the sixties I ran each year about six weekend courses and one summer school on the spiritual themes. Let me tell one strange story. It was on a weekend course on "Light and Love". I gave the final talk on the Sunday afternoon and in closing put on a recording of Beethoven's Hymn of Joy. Then, with an audience of one hundred and fifty, we went into meditation. I had noticed that the cows in the park had all gathered along the sunken fence below the lawn. During the silence they all began to moo and the sheep to bleat and the rooks to caw. There was a tremendous racket and as we went down to tea everyone was saying "Did you hear those cows?" On such an occasion there are bound to be a few real sensitives with 'sight'. They declared that for them the beautiful plasterwork ceiling had melted and disappeared and they saw through into heights of celestial light. In baroque architecture such scenes are painted on the ceilings. Here at Attingham they had the baroque experience in direct vision. They declared that our souls were being drawn or sucked heavenwards through this funnel of Light and that the nature kingdoms were saying "Take us with you, take us with you". Such things may be and our minds must be open to their strangeness!

In these "significant courses" as we called them, many people who are now leading figures in the New Age Movement met each other. We began to know who was in the field. We were beginning to develop an adult education for spiritual knowledge. It was clear that many important movements were already presenting their particular approach to higher knowledge. I now saw the need for a form of adult education which offered the spiritual world-view without commitment to any particular approach.

In 1964 we mounted a conference on "Death and Becoming". This was, as far as I know, the first time death had been dealt with in open adult education. I am proud to realize that at Attingham we held a number of 'first occasions'. There was the very first conference on Teilhard de Chardin to be held in England. I went out to Vezelay to meet René-Mary Parry at the Teilhard conference and invited her to bring her team of lecturers. We packed the house and on the Sunday evening the Teilhard de Chardin Association of Great Britain was founded in my study. We also held the first Psychosynthesis Conference. It was a great moment to be able to introduce the subject to a full house, saying that none of us yet knew what it was, but we were drawn together by the concept of synthesis, which was then in the air.

At this time the holistic world-view was emerging. We now recognize that this world-view involves comprehending that the Earth is a living, sentient being and that humanity is integrally part of nature. Thus conservation is essentially part of the alternative life style, which grows directly out of the spiritual and holistic vision. At Attingham we held a series of ten annual conferences with the Soil Association and the convention was established that I should give a closing fifteen minutes commentary from the spiritual viewpoint. Sometimes this nearly split the Association!

I first visited Findhorn, the community in the north of Scotland, in 1968. I suspected that Peter Caddy's garden of magnificent flowers and glorious vegetables grown on arid sand dunes was the result of co-operation with the nature spirits. For the first time he confessed that this was the truth, so I wrote a memorandum to Lady Eve Balfour which brought up the Soil Association experts to see for themselves. I was never a member of the community, but for ten years was a trustee and felt closely linked. I gave opening lectures at most of their annual conferences which they have published in a little book called *Summons to a High Crusade*.

After ten years at Attingham occurred an event which, being deeply traumatic, served to transform my consciousness. Our lives run with a continuous parallel between outer events and inner development. I have described how the single lecture by Dr Walter Johannes Stein in 1942 lifted me clear of agnosticism and released the spiritual vision. But still it was largely theoretical. By 1958, after ten years at Attingham, I had given many lectures touching on spiritual themes and was learning how to weave this holistic vision into a setting of open adult education. But then in 1958 came an event which was the absolute inner turning point. This was the sudden death in America of my great friend and colleague. Till now my lectures had been based on theoretical understanding, an endeavour to present Steiner's teaching in simple words to the general public, and naturally our attitude to the after-life came in. We were understanding the truth of pre-existence and the implication of Earth as training school for immortal souls in their long education. Now

I had been hit by the event which lifted the whole outlook from theory into direct experience. I now *knew* without any shadow of doubt that the spark of divinity in us cannot possibly die. Therefore the whole quality of my thinking and lecturing was enhanced and lifted. I laughed to think of Samuel Butler's delightful *mis*quotation: "It is better to have loved and lost than never to have *lost* at all."

The great truth is that death in all its forms is the great educator, to teach us that the divine droplet in us always was and always will be. It cannot die and be extinguished. It needs a traumatic experience of loss to make such a breakthrough. Those who have experienced it are the privileged ones. It shows the possibility of establishing a direct contact between the planes of being, not merely   but . This can be the equivalent of the peak experience, bringing about an absolute certainty and subjective proof of the eternal spirit in each of us.

I began a precious little note-book in which to write the names of all our friends who pass over, and whom I know to be in close touch with us, who are working still on this plane for the birth of the New Age. I call it "The Company". The list begins with the name of my friend on 3rd May 1958. This event was a major turning point in my life.

To return to 1971. I now entered a new phase, with burgeoning possibilities! 'Retirement' meant (as so many have found) a release into a new field of activity. We now had 1,500 names on the mailing list for the spiritual conferences. I could not let them down. So with advice from Major Bruce MacManaway, Ian Gordon Brown and Air Marshall Sir Victor Goddard, we conceived the idea of an "Educational Trust concerned with the spiritual nature of man and the universe", to mount conferences all over the country. What was it to be called? I looked out of the window at Attingham and saw our local mountain, the Wrekin and thought: "I will lift up mine eyes unto the hills, from whence cometh my help." I will call it the Wrekin Trust after this central hill in England. And then I remembered the lines from that fragment of an epic by Lord Macaulay, who was my great-great-uncle. He is describing the signal fires leaping from hill to hill to give warning of the approach of the Armada:

> *Till the proud Peak the flag unfurled over Darwin's rocky dales,*
> *Till like volcanoes flared to heaven the stormy hills of Wales,*
> *Till twelve fair counties saw the blaze from Malvern's lonely height,*
> *Till streamed in crimson on the wind the Wrekin's crest of light,*
> *Till Skiddaw saw the fire that burned on Gaunt's embattled pile,*
> *And the red glare on Skiddaw woke the Burghers of Carlisle.*

It seemed we were called on to the adventure of lighting spiritual bonfires on the holy hills of Britain. Here was to be the next phase of work and activity. We wasted no time. In early November we held the first Wrekin Trust conference at the Hayes Centre in Swanwick, on the theme "Death the Great Adventure". It was a tremendous course with a full house of three hundred. This was to be followed by a New Year gathering at Stoke-on-Trent University. At one moment in November my heart sank. Compare the corpse-coloured brick university with our dear Attingham and the great Epiphany festivals we had celebrated there! No one would come. It would be a dismal contrast. But when the time came the place was thronged and it was an inspired course at which J. G. Bennett was chief speaker. At the end we felt those dull brick walls were vibrating with spiritual light!

Ruth Bell, my last secretary at Attingham, agreed to come with me into Wrekin Trust and we established our office in a house in the village of Bomere Heath in Shropshire, near the cottage into which my wife and I had retired.

We now, of course, had no conference house, so we sought out centres in different parts of the country where we could hold our weekend courses. There was now no need for me to be diplomatic and play down my real interest, so I came out in my true colours and proclaimed the spiritual awakening in our time.

Wrekin Trust and Beyond

Throughout my career in adult education I have tried to put into practice Grundvig's *Doctrine of the Living Word*. To me that implied never using notes. I argued that if one needs to look at a bit of paper to find out what one thinks, then the thoughts are not of burning significance. Of course with certain scholarly and more technical or scientific subjects it is necessary to read papers, but this involves the ability to put the subject over as an actor. Churchill was the great example of one who could write out his entire speech and then put it over as if it were spontaneous. For many of us, what is written cold in the study lacks the necessary fire to get over from the platform. The challenge is to speak the living word in a manner that starts a flow of inspiration and is audible to everyone in the room. Thus my lectures at times lost in precision but always came over 'alive'. Having brooded on the subject, I then found that the act of putting it over to the audience started a spontaneous flow of thought. Sometimes it goes off in unexpected directions and has to be brought back into control!

I can see the goal towards which this type of lecturing is leading. It confirms the conviction that there is indeed an ocean of living thought to which our minds are attuned. The brain, we realise, is not so much an organ for secreting thoughts as for reflecting ideas. The Ideas in a true sense, are alive. They are beings, strands of the energy of God. Thus the lecture is not merely a one-man performance. It is a united group endeavour, almost a ritual, in which one is the catalyst through whom living ideas can pour. Thinking is a kind of electrical power, flashing through the group mind of the audience. Thus each lecture can be an adventure, an invocation of the Divine World to speak through human thinking. Grasp that these ideas are living beings, to be seen as energies of God-thought. They long to enter and blend with the layer of human thinking. Once thought on our plane, the ideas are widely available to others.

To Grundvig's "Doctrine of the Living word", I should like to add the *Doctrine of the Living Idea*. Our goal must be to make ourselves worthy instruments for channelling these living ideas. Then a bridge can be made with higher worlds. Here is indeed a clue for exploration into God. It is a theme which will come in throughout this book.

Poetry began to play an ever greater part in my lectures. The poem, after all, is a creation of the right hemisphere of the brain, that gateway to Oneness Vision. Here was a real example of the use of the Living Word. The secret is to teach oneself really to speak living thoughts and not recite dead words. Poetry can be used in active cultivation of Imagination. It was really as if the poets themselves came to contribute to the lectures! So many people asked for copies of poems used that I put them together with a holistic commentary in a little book called: *Magic Casements: the Use of Poetry for the Expanding of Consciousness*

*   *   *   *   *   *

I had been fortunate at Attingham that much of the administrative load had been lifted from me by the Education Department of the County Council, so that I could be continuously engaged in planning and running courses and events. With Wrekin Trust I had the essential need of a colleague who could take over management and financial control. Without such, our position was somewhat precarious. In 1974, three years after launching the Trust, destiny brought that colleague into my life. In midsummer at a conference in London I became aware of a figure I had not seen before, in jeans, bearded, and with an aureole of brown hair. I sought him out in the tea break and he tells me my opening greeting was "It's nice when we meet". I asked him what he was doing tomorrow and he replied "Coming to see you". I am certain that there was here a deep karmic connection and that we had been together in earlier incarnations. I saw in Malcolm Lazarus a wonderful potential and he saw in Wrekin a field of work which could fulfil his capacity. He brought the organizing and management ability and financial experience I sorely needed.

Gradually, in the next years, he learned the arts of planning and running courses and soon became Co-Director of the Trust. Together we mounted and ran some forty residential weekend courses each year and this full flood went on till 1982. Thus Wrekin, in ten great years, had mounted nearly five hundred courses in different parts of Britain and had taken its place as adult education for spiritual knowledge. I owe Malcolm a lasting debt of gratitude and was happy to release full power and control to him as Director.

It was important that we had no label or commitment to any single movement or school of thought. Our task was to present the spiritual world-view in general terms, so that people could awaken to the holistic vision and then find their way to the particular path that suited them best. Thus in the whole wide movement of spiritual awakening and New Age thinking, Wrekin had a special place. We were in touch with all these groups and many of their lecturers spoke from our platforms, but we were not affiliated to any of them. Thus students did not feel that a particular doctrine was being imposed on them, and were free to find their own way.

One of Malcolm's greatest achievements was the devising of an annual conference on "Mystics and Scientists", drawing on to the same platform leading scientists who had arrived at holistic thinking, together with mystics and teachers of spiritual knowledge. At the time of writing this has run for eleven years.

In 1983 it was clearly desirable to pause and give Wrekin something of a sabbatical year. A change in direction was indicated. Now all over the country Networks were emerging, linking local groups founded for study, meditation or healing, or for living the alternative life-style. These really were now presenting the holistic world-view in ways often cheaper than we could do in Wrekin gatherings, hiring expensive conference centres. In the early years we had really been breaking new ground. Now the New Age Movement was forging ahead on a broad front and a stream of books on esoteric and spiritual knowledge was appearing. The Wrekin Trust needed to enter on a new direction and Malcolm saw the opportunity of developing a curriculum of on-going linked courses which really would help people consciously to change and transform themselves. I was very happy at this new stage to make him Director of Wrekin Trust, with myself as Founder/President.

Then, as I approached the age of eighty (in 1986) I invited Tony Neate, the founder of Runnings Park, West Malvern, to become Chairman with his colleague David Furlong as Co-Director. In 1987 Malcolm experienced a time of ill-health, which threw all planning on David. Malcolm also realized that his real task now was to develop his remarkable seminars on "The Transformational Journey". These he had established with his wife Jane and had built up a considerable following. So it became clear to us all that this was the time for him to retire from the Trust. Our long partnership was completed and Wrekin entered a new phase under the inspiration and direction of David Furlong and Tony Neate, with David Middleton as Administrator in charge of the office, which was now moved into the grounds of Runnings Park under the Malverns—a fine centre for spiritual adult-education. I remained as President and for a time, a member of the Trustees.

For me a new phase had been entered—lecture tours on spiritual knowledge all over the country and abroad. This has been my increasing delight in the last years. For twenty-four years I had sat tight at Attingham, like a spider in the centre of my web and had travelled relatively little. Now I saw how many parts of England I had never visited. The lecture tours grew into pilgrimages to explore Britain and go to the cathedrals and sacred centres, while running seminars and giving lectures arranged by local groups. In addition, there have been tours to America, South Africa, the Netherlands, Scandinavia and Germany. Thus I entered the third phase of my post-war quest for the holistic world-view. These tours can now be planned from my home in a converted Cotswold barn.

*   *   *   *   *   *

So there in outline is the story of one man's adventure into the vision of Wholeness, which to me equates with exploration into God. It sounds like a series of unfolding enthusiasms. Inevitably, being a Scorpio, there were traumatic experiences essential to growth of the soul and quenching of the ego, but they need not concern us here. Through the years the conviction grew in me to the point of a deep certainty that the universe is Mind, an ocean of living thought poured out from the Divine source, and that the human entity is a droplet of that Divine mind, which can of its own volition merge with the ocean without losing its identity. There lies the path of spiritual awakening in our time, the evolutionary step which the human being is called on and challenged to take. In this sense we can all begin to "explore into God".

The fact of human freedom does imply that our initiative is an essential factor. Nothing will happen until we take the first step upon the path. Every path will be different, but each leads to the same goal—holistic vision, re-uniting with the Oneness, re-identifying with the Unitary Being of Humanity, which is indeed as aspect of God. So the fact that I am not an advanced mystic or seer may be an encouragement to others to start out on their own journey. Know that we are each in close touch with our own angelic guide and teacher and our Higher Self, who can speak within our own thinking. The door of the prison of self is unlocked. Push it and you can walk through. God is life everywhere, the being that animates all form. The great adventure of our age is indeed "Exploration into God".

Prototypes of Holistic Achievement

WE ARE CONCERNED with the breakthrough to a holistic world-view. We have seen that this is far more than theory. Once it takes possession of us, it brings change in character. We must change. We can no longer go on with the same egoism that characterises the condition of separation. We enter a new epoch, the evolutionary age when human consciousness lifts and expands into an experience of Wholeness.

At the beginning of every epoch certain individuals emerge who have taken the step into the new consciousness. We must think that these are souls who have incarnated in order to lift mankind another step up the ladder—Jacob's ladder. In the Renaissance, Leonardo and Michelangelo were such people. I wish now to speak of two men who appear to have, through their own vision and activity, actually changed themselves and shown the way for others to do the same. These are Rudolf Steiner and F. Matthias Alexander. Each of these in his own way actually brought about in himself an evolutionary transformation of immense significance for the holistic vision and its application to living. It is of course impossible to do justice to the work of such men in one chapter, but since their thinking and its application has been a major factor in my life, I should like to acknowledge and do honour to them in this book.

RUDOLF STEINER (1961–1924)

Steiner's work in researching into the spiritual worlds is of astonishing depth. I am simply concerned here with his approach to thinking as a demonstration of holism.

Indeed, it is highly significant that before he launched out on his teachings about the spiritual nature of man and the universe, he wrote *The Philosophy of Freedom* and *A Theory of Knowledge* about the nature of thinking, to show that his research was by no means the result of mediumship or of higher beings speaking through his consciousness. He wished to establish that he had lifted his thinking beyond the limitations of sense-bound intellect and had in fullest consciousness achieved a oneness with the ocean of Mind, the living Intelligence of the Universe. All his teaching was the expression of direct experience of the spiritual worlds. He was simply describing what he saw and found in these higher worlds and putting it into thoughts for us to understand.

He needed to establish that he had done something with his thinking which had never been achieved before and that his researches into the spiritual worlds had the same validity as scientific exploration of the material plane.

He was born in Austria in 1864 with complete clairvoyance, and the spiritual worlds were fully open to him. As an absolutely first rate scientific mind, teaching the most advanced theories of his time, he saw that his spiritual knowledge was a kind of atavistic throwback into a quite outdated form of thinking, unfitting for a scientific age. Yet this capacity gave him complete certainty about the reality of the spiritual worlds. He wrote of himself:

> *The spiritual world stood self-evident to me. But I felt that it was essential for me to enter it through the doorway of nature. I urged upon myself: "I must intensify my thinking. I must become able with my thinking to penetrate into the reality within natural phenomena. Only in such a way can I legitimately enter the spiritual world."*

He saw that the way evolution had taken humanity, had led to illusion about the material worlds. Our intellectual thinking was based on perceptions through the senses, which were not tuned to apprehend the living being within the forms of nature. He knew by direct vision that these forms were the creation of a world of being, of living ideas which are strands of the ocean of Divine thinking.

Thus he saw that if he could achieve "sense-free thinking", he would be able to unite directly with this world of Being. The way through was clearly by an intense meditative study of nature in her metamorphosis of forms, so that his own thinking could in itself apprehend the thinking of the Universe. If the human ego is a droplet of the Divine mind, then surely this droplet can unite with the ocean of Divine thinking and idea. Thinking thus became the way of research into the higher worlds.

> In this sense man himself holds the key to the secrets of nature. In such concentrated meditation, human thinking is brought into awareness of the creative activity of Thought that lies behind the world of nature.

Once he had made his breakthrough by intensifying his thinking to the point of "sense-free thinking", there was no limit to the possibility of research. He knew he had refuted Kant and demonstrated that in very truth there were no limits to human knowledge.

His teaching life of a quarter of a century in which he gave six thousand lectures, was a demonstration of the human potential of thinking as an instrument of knowledge. Whenever he was asked to speak on a subject, he responded by demonstrating that he could draw knowledge direct from source in fullest consciousness. We are not concerned here to speak of the colossal achievement in sheer work and inspiration. The point I wish to make is that here is a human being who took his own thinking and used it as an instrument for breakthrough into Higher Thinking. He saw that no one before had in this sense considered "thinking about thinking".

The point where ideas bubble into consciousness is, for each of us, unique in the universe. It is the only point where we are, at one and the same time, both creator and observer. The ideas are ours—and yet they are given from an inner, higher source. They bubble up like a fountain of Thoughts, which we can observe. The brain is formed by Thought to reflect the convolutions of Cosmic Thought. My eye cannot see its own seeing, nor my ear hear its hearing, but I can think about thinking. In this humanity is unique, and here we have the clue that opens to us the possibility of exploring the infinite realms of knowledge.

Humanity stands at this threshold. Holistic thinking can grasp this vision. There have of course been seers and initiates in all ages, but Steiner is probably the first to take the conscious step in intensifying his own thinking so that in a clear and scientific manner he could enter the realms of spirit, merging thinking with the Cosmic Intelligence.

Here is an important statement in his autobiography.

> *If we see in thinking the capacity to comprehend more than can be known to the senses, we are forced on to recognize the existence of objects over and above those we experience in sense perception. Such objects are Ideas. In taking possession of the Idea, thinking merges itself into the World Mind. What was working without now works within. Man has become one with the World Being at its highest potency. Such a becoming-realized of the Idea is the true communion of man. Thinking has the same significance for ideas as the eye for light and the ear for sound. It is an organ of perception.*

Thus I submit that here is a human achievement of paramount significance for holistic thinking. A new human species is emerging and Steiner stands as a prototype. We can all follow this lead. In living Thinking lies the key to initiation into higher knowledge, through Imagination, Inspiration and Intuition.

F. MATTHIAS ALEXANDER

Matthias Alexander is another who demonstrated holism, but in a different way. He was not concerned with the spiritual world-view. His discovery concerns the use of the self, the manner in which we direct the way we are using the body as a psycho-physical unity. This achievement started not as a theory but in the tackling of a very practical situation. As a Shakespearean reciter in Australia, he found that his career was threatened through loss of voice. No expert could tell him why this was happening. He then grasped the idea that this defect must be caused by *something he was doing himself* to put the mechanism wrong. Since no one could throw light on this, he got mirrors and watched himself reciting. He soon saw that the greater the effort he put into speaking the more he stiffened his neck and pulled his head back and down, which obviously crushed larynx and the speaking organs. Further that he was dragging his body down, shortening the spine. When he tried to lengthen, he found he dragged the back in, which narrowed the whole rib cage and lung area.

But when he came to apply this discovery, he was completely defeated. Every time he began reciting the same thing happened, because his general habit of use of the whole body had come to feel right. He saw that, if the wrong use of himself felt right, then the right use of the body mechanism would of course feel wrong. He saw clearly that we all rely on the guidance of our feeling, our sensory mechanism, to tell us what we are doing with ourselves. If that kinaesthetic register has become untrusworthy, how can we possibly bring about habit changes in use of ourselves? No one is going to do the thing that feels positively wrong. He was in despair. He knew what he had to do. He had to relax and untense neck and throat, allow the head to go forward and upward instead of dragging it back and down, and thereby maintain the lengthening of the spine rather than shortening it.

This general use of the body mechanism treated as a whole,

would obviously keep the pressure off the larynx and enable him to recite without the harmful tension. But could he do it? Every time he began to recite he found that he followed the guidance of his faulty feeling and reverted to the dragging back of the head and shortening of the spine, because it had come to feel right. Then he made his great discovery. It was so simple, so logical and so very difficult to achieve. Yet here is the holistic clue to taking conscious, constructive control of the use of the body mechanism on which we are dependent in every single thing we do.

He knew that he had found the true and primary movement for each and every act. He came to call it the "primary control". He recognized the holistic nature of the human body, a wonderful instrument which clearly we are constantly misusing because our feeling register becomes untrustworthy. He soon saw in watching himself and others that the tendency was always to stiffen the neck muscles and drag the head backward when effort was made. How often is this apparent in runners straining for the goal. It followed that every attempt at physical training or exercise which did not recognize this primary relationship of parts—head to neck, and head and neck to back as a combined use—would result in loss of coordination of the whole body.

He then made the further discovery, on which the technique was to turn. Whenever I give consent to do something, I tend to stiffen neck and pull head back without knowing I am doing it. I cannot bring about a different use of myself because what is right feels wrong, through habit. Therefore I must learn, when I receive a stimulus, to *withhold reaction, to say NO to the immediate response*. Then I must project a conscious order to my neck to relax and my head to continue in a poised, forward and up direction. Clearly I don't need to *do* anything in order to *undo* tension. It is simply a question of giving an order, sending a mental direction to the neck to relax etc. If the wrong habit comes in every time I try to gain my end, I must obviously cease to be concerned about that end and instead must concentrate on the means whereby I can achieve that end. I must take control by refusing to allow the faulty sensory register to get into action. I must cut out 'end-gaining'.

Once he had mastered this principle and technique he found that the trouble of loss of voice was overcome. He had learned the secret of maintaining co-ordination of the body mechanism, treated as a working whole. The use of the self obviously applied to every action in living. So he devoted the rest of his life to teaching this technique. It is now accepted as an essential factor in the emergence of alternative therapies and life-style.

I want to quote from my diary of 1931 when I first took up Alexander's work and joined the first training course for teachers, in London:

> I went first to see Alexander as an undergraduate at Cambridge. He looked at me, felt me with his hands and said "Young man, what have you been doing to yourself?" He made me make some movements as in fencing, a sport in which I indulged a great deal and with much skill. To my surprise he raised his hands in horror. Then he expounded—I was using myself abominably; I had cultivated unconscious habits which felt quite right but in fact were pulling my poor body out of shape. I was stiffening my neck and pulling my head back; I had got my back pulled right in and it had fixed there as if the framework of the lung was battered in. I was doing these things myself. I was doing them. I myself was positively pulling my body out of shape. Each time I lunged in fencing, in went the back and back came the head. Clearly, the more I did the worse the conditions would become. If in walking I pulled my head back, what must I be doing in the violent efforts of mountaineering! It was suddenly clear as day. Somehow one must stop doing those things which pulled one out of shape to allow the misplaced structures to fall back into their normal conditions.
>
> Here was an idea and a principle diametrically opposed to every exercise or training I had ever heard of. The first lesson was a revelation!. . .

I became quite clear that this technique held something of immense importance for mankind and that I must learn it and be able to teach it. I knew that this was one of the great discoveries. Alexander called his first book *Man's Supreme Inheritance*, his second, *Constructive conscious control of the Individual*, the third, *The Use of the Self* (probably the most useful for study) and the last, *The Universal Constant in Living*.

Those who have engaged in meditation and have also been trained in the Alexander technique will have seen that there is a close parallel. The Tibetan lamas claim the capacity to continue meditation in all they are doing. When we have achieved the poise of Alexander's 'primary control', we can maintain it while giving consent to the limbs doing whatever we want. This has the closest relation to sustained meditation. Non-attachment to 'end-gaining' and control of reaction through 'inhibition' of immediate response to stimuli until directions for the primary control are given, is indeed a kind of western yoga. The act of refusing to respond to the primary desire to gain an end becomes the act of responding to the conscious reasoned desire to employ the means whereby the end may be gained. Clearly and obviously this touches everything we do. Here is the clue for breaking habit and lifting into the new. It would have wonderful effect if it could be included as an essential feature in teaching the 'inner game' of skiing, tennis and athletics. It is as basic to real therapy and healthy living as is nutrition through whole and organic food.

I submit that Alexander demonstrated a principle of supreme importance for a holistic world-view. He made a breakthrough which is nothing less than an evolutionary step forward, when a single human being learned to take constructive, conscious control of the direction of his own use of himself. He discovered man's supreme inheritance and the universal constant in living. He overcame the reliance on faulty sensory register and taught himself a central general habit of use of his entire body working as an indivisible psycho-physical unity.

What seems now to be emerging is a type of human being who is using conscious direction of him/herself. This implies the concept that the body is a potentially perfect tool or instrument for carrying out the purposes of the soul. These two men, Steiner and Alexander, have each in their own way done something which has not been achieved before. They have taken a conscious step in evolution, a step which others will be able to follow. They offer a prototype experience directly relevant to holistic thinking.

Steiner demonstrated the possibility of intensifying thinking so as to blend with the ocean of Mind and explore the supersensible worlds with scientific certainty. Alexander demonstrated how the use of the psycho-physical self can be mastered and maintained, and faulty habit patterns consciously changed.

Steiner showed us how sense-bound thinking leads to illusion and limitation. Alexander revealed that reliance on faulty sensory appreciation will inevitably lead to faulty co-ordination of the whole body and therefore bring about ill-health and impaired functioning.

With our present understanding of reincarnation and the concept of the Earth as training ground for the evolving soul, we can accept that working on the self in these ways will carry its results through from one life to the next. We approach the realization of the archetype which stands before us as the goal, the reality in the Mind of God. Each incarnation will bring us nearer to the achieving of Homo Erectus.

A Further Step
in the Exploration

AT THIS POINT I must introduce a new factor in the personal story. I have, as I said, entered Phase Three of my post-war exploration—first Attingham, then Wrekin Trust and now the lecture tours among the networks. At this stage I met a friend through whom a new step was taken.

It happened like this. My book *A Vision of the Aquarian Age* was taken up by a newly formed publishing firm in America—Stillpoint. Jim Young's colleague as publisher was Caroline Myss. When I visited them in New Jersey, they revealed that Caroline was a sensitive and in touch with her angelic teacher, one who called himself Genesis. We had a session together in which Genesis spoke through Caroline and revealed that he and I had a close link, and that he hoped to have direct touch with me as spiritual teacher and guide. This in fact came about.

Through this Genesis contact I have become ever clearer about the vital truth that the link with the higher worlds is *within our own thinking*. We must not expect to hear outside voices from God and the angelic world. The wonderful and delicate provision is that the higher Source speaks in the still small voice within our own minds. We have become so conditioned to the sense of ourselves as separated onlookers at nature. So long as we go on wanting to hear or see the spirit world as something outside us, the true bridge will never be crossed. By this provision there is no interference with human freedom. No one is constrained to come to God. God is everywhere, everywhen, ubiquitous. He IS the Life animating every form. In man has been evolved a creature with nervous system and brain through which direct contact with higher knowledge and thinking is possible.

I longed for closer direct contact with Genesis—and then saw that he was indeed pooling mind with me and speaking within my own thinking. Mysteriously within the question asked is contained the answer. I took the plunge and began to address myself as from Genesis. At first it seemed a curious process—me talking to me. Then I saw it as the essential next step. I began in dawn meditations to speak very slowly, word by word, into a tape recorder, starting deliberately by saying "George, this is Genesis speaking". It was a tentative beginning, but the results were clearly of a quality beyond my normal thinking. Having spoken for a while, I would play the tape back and let it dictate to me and the slow speech was just the speed to write it down.

We must overcome the sense that it is silly to talk to oneself. What is really happening is that left brain is talking to right brain. The sensitive, intuitive, feminine faculties of the right hemisphere are in direct and immediate touch with the living Oneness. They are the gateway to imaginative vision. The rational left brain relies on sense-bound thinking and, as we have seen, is therefore cut off from the supersensible worlds. We can each in our own way begin to work to establish this link. In a later section of this book I include a number of these conversations with Genesis. They make no claim to be anything very profound. They are perhaps valuable as examples of a way of approach to thinking into the higher worlds and may encourage others to work in like manner.

Communication with Higher Intelligences

It IS ALL VERY WELL to talk about an ocean of Thought and a cosmic Intelligence. That theoretical knowledge alone is not enough. It presents the greatest challenge to the human mind. If ethereal space is filled with intelligence and *intelligences*, spiritual beings who can pool and blend mind stuff, then the implications for us are immense. Communication with higher intelligence must obviously be possible and will be of profound importance in our present world crisis. How do we bridge the gap from separated intellect to pooled consciousness?

We have surely to recognize that thinking is a vehicle for knowledge, if it can be lifted from sense-bound intellect to become a blending with the thinking of beings higher on the Jacob's ladder of the frequency-scale.

In the early days of the Society for Psychical Research the phenomenon of mediumship was explored. Remarkable results were often achieved, but there was always the danger that trance mediumship, involving as it obviously does a lowering of consciousness, could result in deception and even entry of mischievous entities into possession.

Steiner demonstrated through his entire life achievement that it was indeed possible for the human being so to intensify his thinking that he could develop 'sense-free thinking', and thus consciously enter the realm of living ideas. I speak more of this in a later chapter. He made good his claim that there are indeed no limits to human knowledge if this step can be taken, since then it becomes possible to receive from the Source direct answers to any question.

Alice Bailey in all her great books received direct communication from one of the Masters of the Hierarchy, that group of exalted human beings who have achieved higher knowledge and no longer have need for a physical vehicle and yet can take to themselves a bodily vehicle if they so wish. They, it would appear, are overlighting our civilization as it goes through its evolutionary crisis and catharsis. We are watching and experiencing a melting of the barriers between the worlds. The separation of spirit and matter is being overcome. In other words, the reliance on the left hemisphere intellect alone is being modified by the parallel development of the right hemisphere with its feminine and poetical sensitivity.

So many people are now receiving communications from the spiritual worlds. It is a factor which cannot any more be denied. It becomes folly to think that ours is the highest level of intelligence. Holistic thinking must have the courage to take the leap and admit that the human mind can blend with the intelligence of invisible and spiritual and disembodied beings. Examples are now innumerable and only the most obstinate materialist can deny it and remain blind to this fact.

The door lies within our own thinking. This is the wonder. We do not have to wait until the existence of the Higher Worlds can be proven to the logical intellect. We can as from now begin to work to bridge the gap. As I have stressed before, it is not even necessary to 'believe', in the conventional sense of the word. Have the courage to act on the concept that you are a droplet in the ocean of Mind. Activate thinking as an instrument for blending with the Whole. Try it out.

Here is the use of imagination. Remember Keats' statement: "I am certain of nothing but the holiness of the heart's affection and the truth of Imagination." Use mind to call on Mind. This is, of course, dynamic prayer. You are a cell in the body of the living Earth, Terra, the beautiful planet. When you think with love and ardour into the wonder of Wholeness, when you choose to identify with the life that animates the sheath of matter, then you ARE the Earth waking up. Wherever you look, your gaze is met by the forms of nature which your senses can identify. Don't stop there. Let tree, plant, mountain, bird, crystal, tell you of the being dwelling within it and shaping it. It speaks with so subtle a voice to the refinement of your mind and to the listening heart. On *this* level you are one with that being. This experience of Wholeness is one of Joy. You are touched with the fairy wand.

Do not expect to hear a voice from outside booming or shouting or even whispering. Do not strive to see invisible beings. It is WITHIN your consciousness and your thinking that they will work. Only when you have stilled the chattering mind and busy emotion through your own form of meditation can you expect to 'hear' or 'see' in the reflective glass of your own consciousness. It involves a reverential approach to things, a readiness to respond to the Voices of Silence. It needs courage to face the truth that it is within your own thinking that the spiritual beings speak. You have a salutary reticence and doubt about your capacity and a fear of being deceived. Of course delusion and illusion are possible. Ego will always try to get in and have its way. Yet remember this: the theory is that your spiritual guide, your angel or your friend out of the body, longs to be allowed to think in your mind. Invite them. Welcome them. Invoke them. You can always reserve judgment. They always say 'Test the spirits'. Use sound common sense, for you are exploring into a new, strange wonderful realm. But for goodness sake begin! Find your own way. This is the adventure.

Be sure of this, that in this time of travail in the birth of a new humanity, when Planet Earth is suffering and herself praying for redemption, the realms of higher Intelligence will be very close and ready to help wherever they can find entry. The Christ impulse is one of unconditional Love and total and continued forgiveness. Begin with forgiving yourself for your own folly and mistakes and widen out to forgive those around you. God is the Life, which is in all things. Christ is the Love which welds all into a harmony. The desperate things now happening are aspects of the burning out and cauterizing of the evil which we have released.

Here is a sonnet by Gerard Manley Hopkins:

> As kingfishers catch fire, dragonflies draw flame
> As tumbled over rim in roundy wells
> Stones ring; like each tucked string tells, each hung bell's
>
> Bow swung finds tongue to fling out broad its name;
> Each mortal thing does one thing and the same:
> Selves—goes itself: myself it speaks and spells,
> Crying What I do is me: for that I came.
>
> I say more: the just man justices;
> Keeps grace: that keeps all his goings graces;
> Acts in God's eye what in God's eye he is—
> Christ—for Christ plays in ten thousand places,
> Lovely in limbs, and lovely in eyes not his,
> To the Father through the features in men's faces.

Exploring into God in Nature

AGAIN we must adventure into God.

For He IS all things. He is Life. Where we apprehend life, there is God. He is the essence of every thing in Nature. Then how do we find Him? What do we do with our consciousness to make the breakthrough into the 'within' of Nature? To achieve this opening is vital for our present expanding of consciousness. It is an aspect of man's re-vision of Nature to lift beyond sense-bound, matter-bound thinking and apprehend the life, the IDEA, within things. We can all achieve it. It has for me been a vital experience and exploration on my own path, so I offer it simply now.

We can in this section do no more than touch on aspects of Nature to illustrate an approach which will open to mysteries of vision. Clearly there can be no end to human exploration into Nature in this manner. This is the "two-fold and three-fold vision" which William Blake achieved and we can all aspire to. We have to open the inner eye and achieve true vision of what is invisible to normal looking.

Every plant is unique, but all share the same basic stages of growth. Look at that plant. Take it to bits and lay the leaves in series; you will note that the form from a simple beginning passes through its greatest elaboration and then falls back into itself, as if tired of its splendour, until the sepals cluster around the calyx, as if spinning round the stalk. Then appears the corolla of coloured petals. Rational intellect is content to note the form. The imaginative vision apprehends the wonder. Leaf has metamorphosed into coloured petal. A miracle has happened which our normal looking takes for granted. The total quality of substance has transformed, refined, been drenched in colour. As soon as you truly observe the change and indeed move through it with your exact sensory imagination, Mind breaks through.

Nature is a great work of art and design out of the Divine source. We have sensed already that every thing on every level is a facet of the stupendous Whole. Everything interconnects and flows into everything else, while expressing its unique self-hood. And the human being, consummation of the grand design, is the point through which Nature can look and see the divinity within each form. We may conceive that the purpose of the whole Divine Design is that this creature, "a little lower than the angels", shall re-discover God in every thing.

But to it again. Look for examples which in themselves hold the total secret. 'See' them with the heightened vision, which mostly lies in us unused and unawakened. It may be called 'risen thinking'. Such an example: a petal in process of becoming a stamen, may, in Goethe's words, be "worth a thousand, holding everything within itself".

Take the tulip. First the splay of strong fleshy leaves. Then the long stalk from which bursts the crimson corolla. But often enough we see a 'sport', a petal which has appeared half an inch below the coloured flower. It is half red petal and half fleshy green leaf. Tulip hides its secret and then reveals it to the seeing eye. This to you will be absolute proof that the 'being' of the plant metamorphoses green leaf into red petal. We are watching an astonishing secret which reveals what is happening throughout the natural kingdom. Wonder at it. Most of our human art is static—sculpture, painting, architecture. Nature holds the secret of forms which flow into subtler refinement, yet always remain integrated with the Whole.

Now a second example. Take a rose and pick off its petals and lay them in series on a white cloth. The outer first petals may sometimes reveal a relationship to the sepals, but then achieve a perfect shape. Then go on for two or three petals in the series and you find a crinkle in the top of the petal which relates to the beginning of the central rib, and then becomes a kind of hard cyst which then at the next stage reveals a touch of yellow pollen forming. The flanges of the petal then fall away, leaving the rib as a strong stamen with pollen organ at the top. Leaf has metamorphosed through a series of stages to become stamen.

In this chapter we can do no more than introduce this enthralling subject and indicate the way we can watch how nature works. Goethe pointed out the three-fold expansion and contraction in plant forms. First into stem leaf, refining into sepal: then into corolla, contracting into stamen, related to stigma; then expansion into fruit and ultimate contraction into seed.

Take a seed in the palm of the hand and study it closely. Grasp the truth that it is matter returned to complete formlessness. It is 'chaos', in the Greek sense of the word. You do not find the oak tree in miniature in the acorn. Yet the seed, as formlessness, is mysteriously outside time. Wheat seeds from Egyptian tombs have, when planted, been found to grow. That diminutive point is in touch with the Source.

The IDEA of tulip, rose or oaktree, given the right conditions, can pour through the seed-point and manifest the plant cycle.

But here contemplate a decaying log or fallen tree on the leafy floor of the winter forest. That tree stump, once the base of a noble tree, has now lost all its life and, through myriads of micro-organisms, is disintegrating back to soil. A dead log? But it is swarming with living creatures which are busy breaking it down so that it reverts to humus, the matrix of all life, into which the waiting seed can fall, to start the entire cycle once again. Now grasp the great thought. Earth creates nothing. Its function is to break down forms into living soil. The forms are expression of the archetypal ideas which, as we have seen, exist first in the mind of God. The human mind has the capacity, once it is awakened, to apprehend these living ideas within natural forms.

There is a story of the first meeting of Goethe and Schiller at a botanical lecture by Linnaeus. The two poets met outside the lecture room, in deep distress and anger at the dry intellectual approach to analysing nature. Goethe poured out his theory of the archetypal plant. Schiller stopped and said "But this is only an idea". And Goethe thoughtfully replied: "Then thank God I can *see* my ideas with my eyes". At that moment he recognized that in himself had awakened a new faculty of the inner eye, which could directly apprehend the being within the form. This we can all strive to learn and do. This is a form of dynamic thinking through which we can all enter the divinity within nature and experience how it works in the infinite complexity of the wondrous whole. Indeed it is an aspect of 'exploration into God'. The approach has, to me, been a revelation of deep importance.

The best instruction on this approach is to be found in Rudolf Steiner's little book *Knowledge of the Higher Worlds: How is it achieved?* It opens new fields of understanding and spiritual science, since all nature works on the principle of metamorphosis and flow between forms.

What then of the phenomenon of colour in Nature? Steiner has written:

> By experiencing the living element in the flow of colour we come, one might say, out of our own form and share the cosmic life. Colour is the soul of Nature and the whole Cosmos, and by experiencing the life of colour we participate in this soul.

Now a clue to this is found in the conception of Jacob's ladder, the column of frequency bands stretching from the light of the spiritual Sun down to the low vibratory rate of the plane of matter. Though the angels may be portrayed as climbing up and down the ladder, as on the west front of Bath Abbey, the truth is that all rungs are everywhere, all frequencies blending and passing through each other. Many seers have described the marvels of colour on the heavenly planes.

Contemplate that tulip again. Can we realize that the corolla has not only been lifted eighteen inches above the earth? It is truly touching up into a plane of higher frequency. The eye of vision can 'see' that the flowing seas of glorious colour on the higher planes can be touched by the flowers. They are organs which can reach up the frequencies and bring colour into manifestation for the delight of human senses. How dull and prosaic to think you have explained the glory of the flower by saying that its purpose is to attract bees so as to get itself pollenated! Its purpose is to the Glory of God, that the human being, that point of exalted consciousness in nature, can apprehend heavenly colour and 'rejoice in the Lord'. Propagation is essential but it is secondary to the primal wonder of flowers.

In like manner we may consider the amazing symphony of birdsong in the dawn chorus. Ornithological books frequently state that birds sing in order to claim territory. Nature may use the bird-song for that prosaic purpose, but what a paucity of vision to leave it at that! Can we not see that where the advancing wall of light meets and overcomes the darkness of night, nature has created an organ which can pour out divine music in praise of its Creator.

Furthermore the colours of the dawn are the result of the conflict of dark and light. Goethe, again, taught us this splendid concept. Where light shines through obscurity, as when sun shows through mist, the red colour ranges are born. When darkness is covered by lighted obscurity, as when smoke from a cottage rises against dark woods, the blues are born. Goethe spoke of "the deeds and sufferings of light and colour". We may see that, as the Earth turns into the dawn, a wondrous wall of colour and song moves across it to welcome the day with praise. Be not content with the prosaic explanation, true enough but on too mundane a level. Rather grasp that we are born with the faculty of exploring into God and his angels through the lifted vision of the human mind.

PART III

Risen Thinking

The Living Earth—
An Imaginative Experience

"OH YES, we understand the Earth is alive". But there's more to it than that. You can easily get the intellectual concept. What matters is to transform it into an Imagination. Come with me on an imaginative journey.

Go up into the hills. "I will lift up mine eyes unto the hills from whence cometh my help." You are this time in an arid desert valley with grim red crags, parched earth, dry water courses and rocky river bed. Beyond the head of the valley are greater mountains. Hot sun pours down on us and we are thirsty.

Over the higher range allow storm clouds to form, which advance towards us and spread over the clear sky. A damp gust bringing rain. Great single drops first fall in the parched soil and the smell of wet dust and earth is around us. Then the storm. Let it come lashing down, soaking us to the skin. The stream beds fill with first a trickle and then a strong flow of muddy water. Below, in the river bed, a wall of water descends and begins to thunder over the waterfall. Speed up the process and allow the storm to pass.

> For how to the heart's cheering
> The down-dugged ground-hugged grey
> Hovers off, the jay-blue heavens appearing
>   of pied and peeled May!
> Blue-beating and hoary-glow height; or night still higher
> With belled fire and the moth-soft Milky Way.
>
> (Gerard Manley Hopkins)

Crystal clear blue sky with white clouds sailing and a wonderful scent of wet earth around us. And now the miracle (it is perfectly valid to speed up the time sequence, for imagination can over-leap the matter-bound laws of space and time). The first green shoots of grass appear. As we watch, the fields are a'greening (there is no word in our language implying the active process of growing green: in German you can say "Es grünelt"—it greens itself). Grasp the miracle of grass, which can take over the Earth. This simple plant, bearer of life—why green? Why not red or blue grass? Because green is the image of Life. Let the green cover our valley. Let alpine flowers shine in the meadows. The tinkling streams are now crystal clear. Listen to the orchestra of the streams and find out how many 'instruments' you can hear in the music of the waters.

Below us is the forest. Put your consciousness into the great trees. Go down into the roots, invisible to the physical eyes but accessible to the eye of the mind, the imaginative vision. See how the new cells are proliferating according to programmed pattern to grip the rock. Allow the wind to strain the great branches and feel how the roots, with such intelligence, respond to hold the huge structure firmly to the rock. *Intelligences* indeed—we are very close to the elemental beings who are the intelligence of the Living Earth. Of old they called them the gnomes and pictured them as little men with pickaxes and green peaked caps. The simpler country folk would not have differentiated between the outer and inner eye, and the clairvoyants may have confused the two and thought they could actually see the gnomes with the outer vision. And the gnomes would respond by showing themselves in recognisable form singing

Hi ho, . . . hi ho,
As home from work we go . . .

We are getting near to the nature spirits, and the gnomes are the craftsmen who work in the gravity field of rock and crystal. Now 'see' the sap rising under the hard bark and grasp the wonder that here is liquid which should be running ever down to sea level, reversing the process and rising 50, 100 feet up the tree. Of course, the rational scientific explanation is 'capillary attraction'. But that is a name for a process. Behind it is a dynamic factor in the living Earth. The sap is being drawn up by the pull from the circumference—the polar opposite to gravity which we must re-establish as levity. When the tiny green shoot of a tree or flower breaks the hard soil or forces its way through asphalt, you wonder how anything so soft has strength to force its way through. The truth is that it is being sucked up from above. The creation of virgin new cells at that tiny focal point where Life is flooding, can extend to surrounding cells and shape a hole through which the new-forming shoot can be lifted. You begin actually to re-experience this primary polarity of gravity/levity, forgotten for the last two centuries. Go up to the dome of the tree where a million tiny new trees are bursting from node and bud. 'See' that every tree reaches up into a magnetic field that extends invisibly to the far periphery. Experience the entire wood as one gesture of earth expansion. We may even feel that the globe of our own head compares with the globe of the Earth. Are the trees then like the hairs of our head? Then are our hairs something like aerials for reaching out into the life-ocean of space? Think then, with horror, what it will mean when we have cut down all the forests and left the Earth bald. We are working our imagination into the Earth as a living Creature.

We have felt the intelligence of the gnomes. Let us also strive to approach the elemental beings of the water, called the Undines. Look into the miracle of the dew. We have looked at the crystal stream and listened to its music. Let the eye of the mind acknowledge the presence of beings who of course are working in the sap where the downward flow of liquid is reversed to rise in the life of the tree. And in the flowers, the craftsmen are the sylphs or fairies. Of course it is illusion that the physical eyes can see these 'little people'. They are there nonetheless, but the faculties of perception in most of us have gone dormant. Now we begin to overcome the legacy of reductionist rationalism and grasp that with awakened faculties of imaginative perception we can recognize and work with the living intelligences which are the nature spirits. The architects of the plant world are the Devas, angelic beings concerned with the realm where the archetypal Ideas are worked out in the Divine Mind. The craftsmen who fulfil the designs are the elemental nature spirits.

It is good to remind ourselves of the Law of Correspondences. As above so below. As in macrocosm so in microcosm. Since our body, the microcosm, breathes and has its bloodstream and endocrine glands, so in some sense will the macrocosm of the Living Earth. Earth breathes forces and energies. At midwinter Nature has breathed in fully and holds her breath till after Epiphany the sap begins to rise again. At Midsummer she has breathed out to the full and the earth energies stream out into the Cosmos.

At this point we must introduce the concept of Gaia, the Earth Goddess. It was the scientist Lovelock who first resurrected her in his book *The Gaia Hypothesis*, followed by Kit Pedlar's admirably readable book *the Quest for Gaia*. They submit that the concept is really helpful to explain the astonishing intelligence within nature which enabled the Earth Being to defend herself against attacks threatening the harmonious working of the living Whole. It becomes clear that whenever man in his technology threatens to bring about some imbalance, or by massive entropy to bleed the heat-life out of the body of the earth in loss of vital energy, Gaia knows how to counter-attack and in her good time restore the balance. The conclusion is that Gaia must in the long run always win. Mankind, who should be the true steward of the planet, is in fact doing devastating harm in his avarice and ignorance. But Gaia, biding her time, can never be defeated. We speak of 'conquering nature'. In the long run she must overcome us unless we learn to work in true cooperation with her. Perhaps ice-age or flood should be seen as Gaia's ultimate weapons, for she has infinite time ahead of her. What is 90,000 years out of eternity to grind down rock and re-fertilize the depleted top soil for new forests to grow?

Gaia is reacting against her errant steward. The shifting of the continental plates is like Gaia shrugging her shoulders to throw off the irritant of parasite man.

But perhaps it is time to come home from our valley. Know that imagination creates a reality on the subtle planes and that you can go back to your valley when you wish and intensify the imagery and the richness of the experience. Now come gently down and enter again into the cage of the senses, safely barred from the 'menace of eternity'.

Angels and the Living Idea

THE TITLE for the third book in the trilogy might well be "What Really is Happening Now". What, of all that is happening, is real? What is illusion? On what level is the real reality? From all we've been saying, it seems that the most real, most permanent factor, is the IDEA, the Living Thought of the Creator. That came first. That is lasting, not transient, like matter. "In the Beginning was the Word". That great affirmation and meditation in the opening words of St John's Gospel holds the whole secret. In our tumultuous, ever-changing life scene, where nothing seems permanent, we may turn to the Word, the Idea that underlies everything. These Ideas are alive. They are Beings, strands of the thought of God. All is God. God is everything. God is One. Yes, but the multiplicity of the World of Being is reflected in the multiplicity of the natural World, which, bewildering in its complexity, works as a stupendous Unity. We have seen that the IDEA expresses itself (presses out) into visible form and that the human mind can take hold of the idea within each form. This is the wonder. It gives us a new way of looking at Nature, not merely identifying the species of this plant or noting the habits of that bird, but thinking into the Living Idea that animates the form. On *that* level we can become one with the object, for we also are fragments of the great whole.

> *The becoming-realized of the IDEA is the true communion of man.*
> **(Steiner)**

We are a fraction of the whole, yes, but man is that point in nature which has become self-conscious and can think about things and know that he is conscious. Thus the angelic world must delight in looking at nature through our eyes. Think of that! The eye is an organ created by light to see light, just as the ear and its convolutions is made by sound to hear sound. And, further, the human brain is to be seen as an organ for reflecting ideas. It does not secrete thoughts. It is made by thought to reflect thoughts in our consciousness. The convolutions of the brain reflect the convolutions of Cosmic Thought. The globe of the head is a microcosmic counterpart to the macrocosm of the ocean of Intelligence.

Think of the eyes of Nature in all their myriad forms. Modern scientific photography can show us what it is like to look through a fly's eye or an eagle's eye. Some insect eyes are so made that they see all the ultra-violet colours. Yet it must be that Man, the hu-man being made in the image of God, is given an eye which, more than any other, can reflect the wholeness of things. Adam, given the opportunity to name the creatures, was the being who could in his consciousness embrace the lot, the Whole.

The angels and the supersensible beings must enjoy seeing through our eyes and looking at the nature they have created through human vision and consciousness. For them this would be a special form of exploration, bringing them really inside their creation. They can blend with us, as we blend with them. How enriching this would be (will be) when we have made it conscious. We can invite our angel to come on a tour of our world, and in reverse we could journey with him into the supersensible world.

I suppose we should call an angel It, because it is androgynous, a male/female being, yet it sounds so impersonal. If we fall back on 'Him' it must be forgiven, for we are not thinking patriarchally. Here is an important statement by St Augustine:

> *Things were rather in the Angelic Mind than in Nature—that is to say that the Angels perceived and knew all things in their thoughts before they could spring into actual existence. God never works but through them.*

We must come to terms with the concept of the Angels as absolutely real and indeed vital to our existence. It is tragic that such doubt has been thrown upon them. With a gesture of imagination we can come again into contact with these wonderful allies of ours, in the birth of the New Age.

I quote the remarkable poem by Martin Armstrong, called "The Cage", in which he plays with the concept that the five senses are really filters to protect man from the grandeur of the Cosmos.

THE CAGE

Man, afraid to be alive
Shuts his soul in senses five,
From fields of uncreated light
Into the crystal tower of sight,
And from the roaring songs of space
Into the small flesh-carven place
Of the ear, whose cave impounds
Only small and broken sounds,
And to his narrow sense of touch
From strength that held the stars in clutch,
And from the warm, ambrosial spice
Of flowers and fruits of paradise
Into the frail and fitful power
Of sense and tasting, sweet and sour,
And toiling for a sordid wage
There in his self-created cage,
Ah, how safely barred is he
From menace of eternity!

As T. S. Eliot said, "Humankind cannot bear very much reality."

Will you now use imagination to explore out into the higher aspects of the senses. Reach out into the "fields of uncreated Light". Let the consciousness expand into this glory. Listen to the "roaring songs of space". Make the imaginative effort to open to the music of the spheres.

> *Look how the floor of heaven*
> *Is thick inlaid with patines of bright gold.*
> *There's not the smallest orb that thou beholdest*
> *But in his motion like an angel sings,*
> *Still quiring to the young-eyed cherubins.*

You have "strength to hold the stars in clutch".

We are discovering the reality of "ethereal space", that realm outside time and matter, that vast field of Mind, of which the human mind is a droplet. Into this we can expand. It is eternity, which we enter in sleep and when we are released by death, and we can touch in meditation. Touch, we discover, is an extended faculty. The eye-beam, the thought beam, is like a subtler sense organ and the tip of the eyebeam is like an ethereal finger. Use it, knowing that we are where we put our attention. The spiritual world is wherever we are able to apprehend it, and it is everywhere. When we enter ethereal space we can instantly be at the distant stars. Use the thought beam to feel into the subtler realms and so bring back information into your consciousness.

Then the "flowers and fruits of paradise", which with their "warm ambrosial spice" are the ethereal counterpart of our sense of taste and smell. We are realising that our sense organs are actually made by the heavenly realms they can observe. Thus (to quote Goethe):

> *If the eye were not sunlike, it could not behold the sun.*

The complex ear is made by the convolutions of cosmic surroundings—in order to filter "only small and broken sounds". Then what about scent? Does it not imply that on the high frequencies there is an ocean of living scent, and that this has its counterpart in physical matter? The fact that we possess the sense of smell implies the creative field of living scent which we can apprehend.

The artistry of Nature creates forms, but life is then able to metamorphose these into higher and subtler conditions. Thus petal in the flower is leaf metamorphosed. We must feel that the flower is an organism that is reaching up into frequencies far above the heavy material density. All the frequencies are everywhere. Every cubic centimetre is shot through with all that is. Thus the flower, transforming into scented petal, blue, purple, yellow or red, is touching up into an invisible ocean of free, living colour and scent, which our normal senses cannot see or smell. But we are discovering that we have subtler senses and can also refine our coarser sense to apprehend the living Idea and Being working through nature's art of metamorphosis.

Now we must add to the poem the *The Sense of Thought*. The brain, that fabulous organ, the culminating point of cell complexification which can therefore carry the highest consciousness in man, is not an organ for secreting thoughts. It is an organ of perception, for perceiving ideas.

We have realised that there is indeed an ocean of living ideas which are strands of thought and being of God, and to this we can attune. It opens a gateway of exploration into wonder.

> *Let not him that seeks cease from his search until he finds. Finding he shall wonder and wondering he shall enter the Kingdom and in the Kingdom he shall find peace.*

We each of us have our own angel who overlights our lives. They are part of the greater reality. It is of the utmost importance that we should come to terms with this thought. If you like the idea, you can live with it to find out if it is true. 'Belief' is not demanded. Thought is invited.

This then is the concept. The angels are living beings, strands of the thought of God. They are energies that are so alive that they can embody themselves in form. They are the living Ideas or archetypes with which creation begins. They were explored by Moses during his years of revelation in the wilderness. His findings were confirmed by Dionysus in recognising the nine hierarchies of the Heavens. These great beings exist on many levels, from the exalted seraphim and cherubim, close to the throne of God, down to the individual angels whose primary task is watching over humanity and helping our evolution to fulfil itself.

Thus in our epoch the concern of the angels with our world will be very great. We stand at the threshold over which we may step into the width of cosmic consciousness. This is a culmination of aeons of evolution. Our generation is privileged to be involved with this tremendous challenge. We have discovered that the prison door is not locked and all we have to do is to push it open and walk out, beyond the cage of sense-bound, matter-bound thinking.

Humanity, carrying the precious gift of free will, has a great and wonderful task. We approach a time of initiation for the planet and for our race, when consciousness can take a forward step and blend with the beings of the higher worlds.

For long ages our angel has watched over us and we have totally ignored It. Now we must put right that omission. Here is a little poem by Christian Morgenstern, translated from the German:

THE ANGEL

Oh, if only you knew how much your countenance changes
If in the middle of a glance (the still and pure one
   which united you to me)
You lose your inner self and sweep away from me,
As a landscape, bright just now,
Clouds over and locks me out from you.
Then I am waiting, waiting silently
Often long, and were I a man like you
   the torture of my scorned love would kill me.
But the Father gave me endless patience,
and, unshakeably, I wait for you.
I wait for you whenever you will come.

Take this mild reproach as no reproach—
as a chaste message only.

Our angel works closely with our higher Self in staging situations for our education and testing. Our life on Earth is an initiation and we are given ordeals and trials. If once we really grasp this, we shall accept our difficulties and apparent misfortunes as part of the great plan, and give thanks for them. After all, our temporary sojourn on the planet is but a short parenthesis out of the greater existence in the spiritual world. Furthermore, since we are immortal and imperishable beings, we have the whole of eternity for our exploration and development. We come from God and after the experience of separation, work back into Him as conscious beings.

The angels do not need freedom in the human sense. They are integrally one with the thought and being of the Creator, differentiated indeed, but blended always with the Whole and their delight is to serve that Divine Whole. Humanity "a little lower than the angels but crowned with glory and honour", has a place of great privilege in the pattern of the universe. The 'Tenth Hierarchy' has been given the opportunity of developing free choice and therefore coming back to the Father as a conscious co-creator. This beautiful Planet Earth is the setting for the great experiment of a part of creation which itself becomes creative. Therefore the Heaven World watches this planet with great interest, for it is truly a seed point from which can come something new into the universe.

Angels obey. Their delight is to fulfil the will of God. They will never impose their will on the human being, for they must respect our freedom. The human 'I' is divine. It is a droplet of God. Therefore we are in the position of being *entitled* to call on our angel and give our orders. Though they are in a sense 'higher' than man, we have a very special position as creator with freedom of choice. Therefore we must assume that our invisible angel is present instantly whenever we think of it and that it will obey our behest, for its task is to serve.

Don't wait with hope that some day you may 'see' your angel. Accept its reality and call on it—often, for this is its delight. Whenever you drive a car put your angel up in front to protect you from accident. Do not feel it is trivial to ask it to find you a parking place! Once you start on this game, watch how frequently it works. The apparent coincidences are probably examples of angelic co-operation. Use imagination. You won't 'see' an angel with your physical eyes, but you can validly *think* it, and indeed see it with the 'eye of the mind'. Imagine it and place it at your bedhead when you go to sleep or take it walking through the wood. Love it, welcome it, acknowledge it and apologise for the long neglect of which you have been guilty. Always thank it when you dismiss it. We have to take the initiative in playing this game of angels. Until we start, nothing will happen. If you like the idea, get going and talk to your invisible companion and bring it into your counsels. Since it is alive, it will respond to you by bringing an inner certainty into your consciousness. This is healing: this is wholeness. It is 'wholesome'. (What a good word!) A joy will begin to flow between you and it.

We recognise Joy as an aspect of God. There is the sudden impulse of glee in the heart, that rivulet of enthusiasm (which means 'possessed of a God'). Learn to notice those moments, for they are the flowing of the divine current. Just conceive of the ecstasy when you are free of the limitations of sense and substance and can truly blend with other beings.

Now take the step in thought of knowing that you have an Angel, a loving being who is concerned with your progress and has been allotted the task of watching over your life. Sceptical humanity has cut this factor out, because of the inability actually to see these invisible beings. Apply now the principle we have often stressed—you don't need to 'believe' but, if you are attracted to the idea, you are invited to *think* it and act as if it were true. Call on that angel and 'know' that instantly it is there, your loving helper, servant and guide.

It will never impose itself. Like any good and loyal servant, it waits in the background until its master calls. It is the perfect Jeeves, who knows the answer and can help in all situations for, being semi-free, it has a wider view. But it will never interfere with your freedom. That is the Divine Instruction. Therefore nothing will happen between you until you take the initiative. You are fully entitled to order and command the angels. Though they have a width of knowledge which is beyond us, we also have something that they have not got: we are able to act creatively to shape events. The angelic world stands alerted to help in the great transition into cosmic consciousness.

Be perfectly practical. Begin now to act with your angel. Constantly give it orders, instructions, love and thanks. Be grateful and humble for the thought of how long you have gone on ignoring this patient, generous, loving creature, who has taken on the task of looking after you. No tasks are too small for it to be prepared to help. Above all, know that it gives you protection. It can form a protective force-field in your aura. It can help you to solve your problems. The angel can act as guard to you in dangerous situations, but is unable to act unless you have given the order and thus must stand by and watch while you are thrown into confusion by some difficult circumstances. But always remember that it will not advise you what to do. The choice is left to you.

The important thing now is to establish the habit of mental co-operation. Give it the assurance that you know of its presence and value it. Call on it and then act into the new.

Remember that the angel works with your Higher Self to stage situations for trial, testing and initiation. Then at the moment of decision it steps back and folds its wings and will give you no hint as to the course you should take. It respects the freedom of its master. *You*, not it, are in command.

Your friends out of the body also respond immediately when you call them. They, with the angels, operate in the region outside time. They occupy ethereal space and therefore can be instantly wherever they direct their attention. But they too will not interfere until you ask them. Ask and it shall be given to you. Seek and ye shall find. Knock and it shall be opened to you!

Get knocking! Get asking! Here are your allies so long ignored. A joy floods through the angelic realm as more and more human beings awaken to the reality of angel guides and actively call upon them. It is a lovely companionship.

Let me end this chapter with a Findhorn story. A young woman in Germany, an advanced sensitive, was guided to go to Findhorn. She had no knowledge of the place or what was expected of her. She arrived at the time of a great conference and it happened that I was to give the opening talk in the Universal Hall. This is a splendid five-sided chamber. At the beginning I called on the angels and placed one in each of the five corners. After the event we dispersed for tea and bed. When the throng had gone, this lady came to Peter Caddy in consternation, declaring that a terrible thing had happened— Sir George had ordered the angels to take their stand, but had not dismissed or thanked them! Like good soldiers they continued their watch. So Peter and the lady and a few others had a small ceremony of dismissal, and next morning I brought the conference together again to make a formal apology and gesture of thanks and understanding, and our German friend was then satisfied! So were the angels.

We are relating to an invisible world and must learn the rules by which we must work. Finally remember the power of creative imagining. We may, and indeed must, take the initiative of imagining a light-filled being, calling on it and placing it in position, even though we cannot yet 'see' it. Think it. Imagine it, knowing that imagination is truly a creative process. All this about our relation to the angels should become a factor of ever increasing meaning and joy in our lives. Love them and give thanks when you dismiss them. They are a wonderful and vital factor in the coming of a new age. The relationship will deepen until more and more people are really able to converse with them.

What are we Educating our Young People for?

THIS INDEED IS a vital question. Many of our young are in doubt as to whether they will be alive in ten years' time. Will there be jobs? Or food? Or will dramatic earth-changes have altered the world? Is it worth working for a qualification?

In our dramatic age it is important consciously to educate for change. We need to develop in our young people a quality of creative readiness to adapt and to face totally new situations. How do you learn to move into the unknown with confidence and courage? If the rational, materialist viewpoint were the only truth, then indeed we could rightly feel bewildered and anxious. But we know that each one of us is overlighted by a Higher Self and a guardian angel-guide. This is vital information. It is a factor with which we must learn to work. Our educational approach must first give an understanding of the holistic and spiritual vision. Learn to conceive and grasp that the Earth is a vibrant living being, that Gaia, the Earth Goddess, is a reality of intelligence in Nature, that the human being is integrally part of the whole, indeed that point where nature can break through in consciousness and think God's thoughts again. This opens the possibility for the mind to traverse the living Universe and experience the fact that it is truly a strand of the great Totality. A sea of Intelligence pervades all space and, in all its infinite diversity, operates as a great Oneness.

Teach the young person that this is not rigid dogma to be believed. Indeed, 'belief' is not necessary, for our challenge is to explore a realm of living Ideas and learn to think them and act into them. The logical, rational, left hemisphere of the brain, working with the physical senses, can explore the realm of matter. Indeed it has reached the frontier over which it must bravely pass to apprehend the reality of creative spirit.

But the right hemisphere of the brain, the more feminine faculties, are attuned to the living, light-filled Whole. Therefore the thinking of the right brain is like a spring or fountain welling up out of the eternal worlds. The nature of a spring is that you cannot possibly know what is going to flow forth until it has emerged. So with thinking. You are, in that right brain, in direct touch with the spiritual heights. Thus this is the true organ for poetry, in the attempt to allow expression of the deeper truths of nature and of life. The rational, left-hemisphere thinking can observe this flow of living thought.

We can apprehend the truth that first in creation are the archetypal ideas of each thing or species. These constitute the ocean of intelligence filling ethereal space. We can grasp that every material object and living form in nature is the expression of an archetypal divine idea. This of course, is quite hidden to sense-bound thinking. The great and royal privilege and power of mind is to apprehend the secret and learn to know the being within the form, the idea that inhabits and works in each and every thing. Here is an advanced task for every mind to tackle. It clearly goes far beyond usual natural history or scientific observation. It involves the awakening of a latent faculty for spiritual perception, a way of thinking and observing so that we may 'see' in our lifted thinking the invisible creative being which operates in the form.

A poetical wonder emerges as we learn to look in this deeper and higher way. We do not 'see' the spiritual worlds with physical eyes. Indeed, these worlds are not outside of ourselves. It needs an imaginative leap to grasp that the human vision can equate with the totality. The higher realms and entities speak to us *within our own thinking*. One begins to see in inner apprehension. To this wonderful process there is no end. It gives the clue as to how the human being can explore higher worlds, and enter into the realms of creative being which have poured themselves forth into the world of nature. We grasp that we human beings are that part of nature which has reached the point of making the leap into wider consciousness, crossing the ether frontiers where take origin far subtler systems, nobler regions, for our understanding.

Here we see a field of educational training so that the young person can begin to grasp the oneness of all life and the true kinship of the human being with Nature in all her varied forms. It opens endless fields of exploration. Intellect and intelligence are called on now to explore across these subtler frontiers, so that the human being may truly take his/her place as the crown of nature and the vehicle for new and far wider consciousness and apprehension.

Now to a very practical point for advancing education. We admit that we shall in the coming years all be faced with situations that have no human precedent. We are much used to reacting to stimuli along habitual brain tracks and habit patterns. The animal world entirely relies on such reactions through the wondrous workings of instinct. If the human being is to survive in the coming world conditions, he/she must be able to react into quite unknown conditions for which there are no habit patterns.

Here we touch a major need in educational theory and practice. And here is a vital clue which we can understand once we accept the reality of our higher self and angel guide. These beings are perpetually staging situations for our testing and education, using the outer conditions of our lives to teach vital lessons. They will never impose upon the human being. Clearly that has been forbidden by divine command, for mankind on earth is the great experiment of developing a species which can in freedom come back to God as co-creator and friend. This is the wonderful purpose of life on earth. Naturally the fallen angels strive to drag man down and to deny God. They have no compunction about direct attack to get hold of human will and thinking. Armageddon has been joined, but the forces of the Light under the Christ and Michael may not interfere or enforce co-operation. We have each to reach the point of voluntary dedication of all we are to the Divine Service and the adventure into higher consciousness. Thus our Higher Self, having staged a situation for choice and action, will step back and leave the decision entirely to us. We then have the choice of acting into the Whole as co-creator or of reverting to the desires of ego and our separated selves. Here we touch the great adventure of our time. We can learn, so to speak, to dance with destiny, moment to moment, living in the eternal Now. Since Higher Self is outside our time scale, operating always in the immediate instant, it can respond to our bold reaction into wholeness and on that instant flood us with fresh creative response and energy. Here is the clue for *acting* into the totally unknown. It will need courage and alert attention. When a human being achieves this flow, a new quality of humanity must manifest.

Out of the confusion of a crumbling society will emerge individuals who are touched by this higher guidance. These will inevitably flow together with others of like inspiration, and a new quality of society will begin to form. This is the true adventure of our time.

Teach it. It is not dogma to be enforced. But the young can (and must) be given the opportunity to understand and experience how close to them is this guidance and companionship. An educational system could be built upon this vision of the creative drive out of the Whole.

BODILY EXTENSION

A Sonnet by Charles James Earle

The body is not bounded by its skin:
   Its effluence, like a gentle cloud of scent,
   Is wide into the air diffused, and blent
With elements unseen, its way doth win
To ether frontiers where take origin
   Far subtler systems, nobler regions meant
   To be the area and the instrument
Of operations ever to begin
Anew and never end. Thus every man
   Wears as his robe the garment of the sky—
So close his union with the cosmic plan,
   So perfectly he pierces low and high,
Reaching as far in space as creature can
   And co-extending with immensity.

Risen Thinking

I HAVE SEEN the vastness of the One. Wholeness, Life, Thought, Intelligence as a great ocean, ever pulsating, all interweaving. It is all alive. The Source has poured it forth and it can create forms, myriad forms, all in transformation and metamorphosis.

Among those forms it creates one—Humanity—which by complex sensitivity can become conscious of the great process. For this we need to be able to think, to feel, to have volition. We have in this sense to be separated off from the One, though of course we are still integrally part of it.

But such an organism, an Ego, has needs and desires. That it may survive, it develops an instinct of self-preservation. Yet its real purpose, its ultimate goal, is to become a *conscious* part of the Whole. Then it would have the potential of all knowledge. It can project its attention to any part of the Whole. Planet Earth has been chosen as the ground for this experiment. It is a very rare and beautiful planet. It may even be that Humanity, itself a cellular organism floating in the sea of Life, found and chose this planet for its home.

Here, however, egoism became rampant. Fanned by the adversary beings, the satanic rivals of God, we became primarily concerned with satisfying desire and gaining power and wealth.

Deeper intuition, that essentially feminine faculty, originally gave us some feeling for the living oneness. Early civilizations had a quality of matriarchy. We now know this is associated with the right hemisphere of the brain.

But the left hemisphere faculties, the masculine organising intellect, perfect instrument for control, became dominant. Worked upon by the tempters, patriarchal societies developed concerned with getting all they could for themselves. They lost the sense of the living oneness.

Initiation is the mystery of restoring the sense of oneness, of actual experiencing in consciousness that we are each a droplet of Divinity that can know the One.

Here we are now, errant stewards of the planet, rapidly destroying this beautiful home in our greed and ignorance. There is still time—perhaps! A sufficient number of human beings must stop and make the inner turnabout in consciousness, in self-transformation, so that each can experience itself as a cell of the huge Whole.

This initiates a process, a kind of ferment working like yeast through the human layer. We need not be abashed at our smallness and weakness. Think only of the tiny, fertilized cell which grows into a human being, or the acorn that grows into a mighty oak.

Then that grown being discovers himself/herself as a cell in the greater Whole. But more: that Whole is alive. We float, always, and inevitably in a matrix of life. This life is also divine intelligence. Within the divine mind is a drive to realize the harmony, an impulse of love, capable of a self-cleansing process. This is going on now.

These angelic beings are of the nature of living thoughts of God. They are strands of the outpoured ocean of His thinking. Thus the world process *is* Thinking. We human beings, operating from a body, experience separation. Brain gives us intellect, but this intensifies the sense of apartness. Yet clearly to blend with the angelic world is a thinking process. Our sense-bound thinking with which we operate in embodiment, is obviously fallible. But if we could lift into sense-free thinking and receive the angelic beings in our minds, we should be getting absolutely direct truth. We have got to learn how to achieve such thinking and to trust it.

We have been cut off. We must re-establish contact and become one with the One. We stand on the threshold of a modern initiation. Once this bridge is achieved, we shall be able to explore higher worlds in our thinking. This truly is Exploration into God, for the source is everywhere and in everything, always.

PART IV

*Adventures
in Imagination
and Channelling*

The Escape

How OFTEN warfare gives images that speak to us. We are like a resistance movement in enemy occupied country. Our task is to create centres and groups linked in a network. We can use significant points in the countryside suitable for landing from the air. The coming invasion has been announced. The time is imminent. We have to be in position to signal up to the invading force.

Another image—we are prisoners in a concentration camp. We have descended into the world of matter, captured there and cut off from all contact with our original home and sphere of activity. Many have come to feel that there is no other plane but that of matter and that it is the primary reality. Now continuous signals are coming through to us that such a world of light does indeed exist and that we can escape and find our way back to it.

Now, the prison camp is the time-and-matter-bound life. We are caught by past and future—regrets, remorse, guilt, disappointment, sense of opportunities missed or bungled in the past. We are filled with fears about the future. The forces of darkness want just that. So long as our thinking is tied down to past and future, they have got us.

The prison door is this immediate NOW. Push it and walk through. But obviously the now is always moving on. It is the point where God's presence is contacted. It is the intersection point of the timeless with time. But the only way to move through it is to abandon self and lower ego, with its ties and desires. These must be jettisoned. You can only travel very light—into lightness. You can't take all the luggage.

Outside and above, the invisible guide is waiting. He can speak in your thinking with the still small voice. He can use your faculty of intuition to suggest to you a course of action into your higher Self. You have in this escape got to rely entirely on this intuition and obey it implicitly. There will be no time for reasoning intellect. Split second decisions will be essential, and your intuition, God-filled, will be your guide.

If we can learn to work with it as it speaks in the heart, we have the Ariadne thread which will lead us safely through the labyrinth.

The presence of God is, axiomatically, everywhere. Every situation is an aspect of the total Oneness. Therefore it follows that the necessary information for the next step is always there. The higher Self obviously has an overview of the general situation and can guide you through the labyrinth, one step at a time. But this implies abandonment of self to Self, throwing yourself on Providence. What an adventure! Indeed, it is *The* Adventure of our time! The situation in the Prison Camp is so grave, grim and ghastly that it is worth the risk of attempting the escape. Come on! Let's go! Push that door and it swings open.

This is going to involve a sort of reckless gaiety of response, a dancing with destiny moment to moment. The higher self will suggest courses of action which you have never followed before, since you normally revert to old habit patterns and brain tracks. So you are truly acting into the unknown, faced with situations which call for reaction in ways you have never before experienced. But the assurance is that the higher Self, which loves and watches you (and truly IS you, the God in you) is always present. He, IT, will whenever you call put a forcefield of light and protective power around you. This, if you can maintain it, will give you complete protection from the guard dogs or the bullets of the guards. It will even make you invisible to them, for it is a sheath of very high solar frequency. Yet to maintain it is not easy. If you revert to the old thought vibration of fear and guilt, the forcefield will disperse. You cannot operate with the two frequencies at the same moment. Every moment of choice offers you different courses of action.

The way through the maze is to choose the course which makes most for wholeness, your own wholeness and your conscious relation to the greater Oneness of Life. You must be prepared to follow that course whatever it asks of you. By no means will it always be what your ego thinks it likes, but you are not now concerned with satisfying desire or personal pleasure. You are on the adventure of escape and return home to the great Oneness to which you really belong. This is so exciting and rewarding that it is worth sacrificing all the old habit patterns and ways of doing things.

You know very well that you have, as a human being, been granted freedom. You are not, like the angels, integrally part of the Will of God. Their joy is simply to serve that Will all the time and to obey it. Yours is consciously to take control of yourself and move creatively with the new. Therefore you will constantly be faced with choices, which in fact are situations staged by your higher self for your trial and training. You are led to the point of choice and then your Guides step back and leave the decision entirely to you. But they are watching. If in freedom you choose the course that makes for wholeness, they can instantly pour energy through you, and you will find you have acted in ways you have never before conceived. If in fact you take the more timid choice and revert to the old habit pattern, they will somehow check and reprove you and stage another opportunity. The free choice is always yours, but you have the assurance of their loving concern and inner guidance. It all turns on the motive. If this genuinely is an effort on your part to serve God and progress towards greater Unity and Love, then the slight mistakes are of little significance.

If the inner motive is still self, its power and pleasure and gain, then you will suffer for it and build up more bad karma to be cleared at some later stage. So get moving on the escape.

The Voyage in
the Little Boat

"THE SUN SOUL enkindle us with holy fire. In my head live your thinking and bear spiritual beings." Oh wonder, here is the great truth. Here is the gateway. Speak *in* my thinking. If we are blended, then that which my mind thinks is You and behind you the Christ power.

We are many, yet one. We float in that ocean of living thought. We are operative, yet serving. We can initiate, yet in so doing we enhance the One, the Whole.

Our initiative is obviously vital. *I* have to make the start. I am at present drifting around in separation, a little bit of life which is following its own desires and fears and sense of guilt or disappointment, or its personal ambition.

Will you note that *sense of guilt*, an aspect of the senses. There is indeed a sense of collective guilt to which we can open ourselves. We have a sense of sight made by the light, a sense of hearing which forms the receptive ear, a sense of guilt formed by the huge all-pervading sea of guilt, a sense of fear created by the great illusion.

But we are each this spark of divinity, of God. Right; stop in this moment. This Now. There is only one Now. All the rest is the illusion of past or future. Now, flowing into the next Now, a continuous flowing.

Your little boat rocking, bouncing, on the current. Look what you've been doing, you've let the rudder go! You've been simply washed around by currents of doubt, of fear, of disappointment, of remorse, of timidity; you've let yourself be a victim of every flow that hits you. Get up, take hold of the tiller. Right. Begin to control the direction. You are in control in the Now. Your boat is very small, yes, but it is buoyant.

We take the current and now truly flow with it, in control. Take hold of the sheet, shake out the sail and now what happens? the wind comes into the sail.

> *Not I, not I, but the wind that blows through me.*
> *A fine wind is blowing the new direction of time.*
> *If only I let it bear me, carry me,*
> *If only I am sensitive, subtle, oh! delicate, a winged gift,*
> *If only, most lovely of all I yield myself and am borrowed*
> *By the fine fine wind that takes its course through the*
> *   chaos of the world.*

(from D.H. Lawrence "Song of a Man who has Come Through")

This is the game. The wind of the Spirit is blowing. Look how it is wrecking the boats, driving the ships hither and thither. Look how some of them have taken over and have crews that control the sails and the tillers. Some are going purposefully. Some are merely washed around and sinking. You are responsible for your little boat. The wind is the wind of the spirit, the transforming, cleansing power of the living Christ, the Christ of Light, the Christ of Love, the Lord of Life.

Blow, wind of God. Think; in this moment you can choose to cut out negative emotions, can you not? For the moment as you sit, you inhibit instant reaction, all the fretful desires to do this or that. To that you say No and you go into the relaxation of meditation. Then you inhibit thought, by concentrating upon the breathing. By drawing down serenity into your soul, you exclude thoughts of fear, anger, disappointment, alarm, disturbance, anxiety, dislike of others.

For today, for this little voyage, you will simply exclude the negative thoughts which are all concerned with past regrets and future fears. You will strive to live in this moment, in your little boat, controlling sheet and tiller as you cross the lake and move with the current into the greater river.

Will you now grasp the concept of using 'The Perfect Language'? You will cut out from your vocabulary any words or thoughts associated with the negative emotions. Simply refuse to use them, and watch that you use only a vocabulary of courage, sympathy, joy, tenderness, love, hope. Remember that you *are* the vocabulary you use. As you think, so you are. If you for this day do not speak any negative word or thought, you are well on the way to excluding such thoughts from your mind and soul. Put them aside. Every gust of wind which hits your sail and threatens to drive you off course, you meet by your control of the tiller and sheet, so that you turn it into something which helps you towards your goal. Let the winds blow; you have taken control of sail and rudder and can make use of every wind. You become the thoughts you use and allow. If you never make use of the negative thought you are well on the way to becoming a being of love, and remember that these positive attributes are the Christ Love, Light, Life. But begin by simply cutting out from your vocabulary all the words of negative emotion, bitterness, hate, anger, sarcasm, criticism, scandal and the like.

You open yourself to the inflow, through-flow of the positive qualities. So you will become. If you don't take the initiative, nothing will happen except the uncontrolled drive towards the rocks or sandbanks.

You have taken the tiller, you have held the sheet to control the sail. That which was driving you towards shipwreck now becomes a constructive force through which you advance towards your unknown goal. Claim your Christhood. Christ *is* the force of love, of non-violence, of compassion and tenderness, the sense of Oneness of all beings in all their diversity, the life, the same life that flows through everything. Claim it. Be it. Let It be You.

Just think what will happen when soul after soul has taken this step. Look how blended souls become groups. larger boats are structured across the ocean of life, a whole fleet begins to sail, little boats, big boats, small groups, great organisations dedicated to the Christ power, serving, controlling the progress forward, using the winds of God for progress. A new Armada, indeed.

Take control, take command, raise the banner of Christ/Michael to the masthead. Go into action for Him. Look at the earth with the eye of imagination and see the spreading of this consciousness, of this initiative. Where this power of Life, Light, Love is allowed to enter the human layer, that layer begins to glow.

Stand outside the planet and look at it. See the Earth becoming luminous—this murky darkened planet in which storms of sinister emotion, hurricanes of violence, typhoons of terror, are sweeping through the human layer, this dark and dying planet. Look down now with satellite's eye, at the picture of the weather. Do you not have two forces playing into each other? One the low pressure, the negative, the storm forces carrying sleet and snow and hurricanes, destructive and dark weather, and the vortices of high pressure, bringing the sun, the tranquillity, the gentle breezes.

See that each human centre is a tiny vortex which can join together with other vortices and can have free choice. Either make the low atmospheric pressure, or join the high pressure. It is a dynamic process, part of living Earth, for atmospheric change is surely a picture of the breathing of the living earth, drawing into itself sunlight or rain. Thus we are looking at a psychic atmosphere of the earth, in which the human being, each one of us, is a factor. Decide to take part in the coming of the high pressure.

Open to the glory of sunlight and fair weather. As the warm front advances, the Earth becomes luminous and is beginning to glow. Imagine this. It is valid that you should use creative imagination. See the whole planet in which these centres of light begin to merge with each other, and great areas of the dying darkened planet begin once more to be vibrantly alive.

The Christ power *is* Life. The life that is in all things is one Life, one Spirit, and the human hierarchy is called upon to awaken, to become active, to take the initiative to enable this Light-Love force to penetrate the whole of nature.

The initiative perforce must come from the individual, from each of us, but in immediate response, the higher intelligence, the power of the Christ and the angelic world, can flood in energy. It is a wondrous process. When a certain stage has been reached, the whole planet will be flooded with light. It is a storm. This power of the wind of God can drive the uncontrolled, the negative, the cruel, the brutal, on to the shoals and rocks. Humanity *is* the factor, that point within living nature, in which nature can open to the true flooding of a power of harmony—a power of love, which means that every particle of life in all its diversity knows itself to be working as part of the living Whole. Everyone is of value, none is too small or insignificant to take part in this wonderful operation, which is nothing less than the transformation of the planet. All are called on now.

Take that rudder. Set sail. Realise that *you are what you think*. As a man thinketh so he is. In your thinking the beings of the higher world can become operative. It is a wonderful process, for you are not going to *hear* a voice which speaks out of God. You are going to hear your own thoughts, but those thoughts can be impregnated by the thoughts of your guide. Always they are *your* thoughts. You experience the God-thought in your own thinking as if you had thought it yourself. Therefore you have no obligation to follow it. It is not interfering with your freedom. Do not fear being taken over by darker spirits, for, remember that these negative, adversary beings work in the emotions of fear, hate, anger, criticism, discouragement, negativity, cynicism.

If you have accepted and are ready to use the "perfect language" and are cutting out these negative words and thoughts, emotions and attitudes, how can the darker beings take possession of you? The Christ is never cynical, never enters into negative criticism, never constrains, never hates. For He *is* Love, He *is* Oneness. Therefore if within yourself you allow only the thoughts, attitudes and emotions of joy, calm, tranquillity, serenity, and non-violence, you are making of yourself a channel for the living Christ.

Go forward therefore into joy. Invite your guide, your angelic friend, filled with the Christ Love, to come down on to this earth plane. You will have made the planet glow a little lighter. You will have become a luminous point and you will draw to yourself not only the groupings of human souls also on this path, but you send up a little beam which draws down ethereal light and power. The angelic worlds can then respond. They see this light, a little light which cannot be hid, and they know that here they may flood into the darkened earth plane.

These infinite numbers of little lights together lead to the becoming luminous of the whole planet, a force which is stronger than the powers of darkness. Darkness cannot live where there is light.

Draw down the light. This is your task. Set forth in that little boat with joy and with the flag of Christ/Michael at the masthead. This is the message for the day. Fare forward, traveller.

U.F.O. Experience

THERE IS A SPACESHIP landed in the forest. Its doors are open, and within is effulgent light. There are beings who emerge from the depths of the light, quite impregnated with its quality, beings of light. We are invited in, we are drawn in. One goes before me and the body becomes translucent, glowing. Some will not go in. There is no need to. But I can see that for one who does, that which is of darkness or negativity must have been expunged. It is thrown out by the radiation of this light. It is, therefore, not possible to enter unless that which is negative—fear, criticism, guilt, hate, doubt are relinquished. It is a process of cleansing, a kind of bath in light.

We are dressed in an etheric robe of seamless white. We carry a golden cross hanging over the heart centre and a circlet with a star over the brow centre. My turn comes to go forward. Let me be worthy of this, for it is an initiation. I walk up to the doors of the ship, which is the usual circular UFO form. I am met with a powerful radiation of warmth and light. It is a cleansing. On my part, there can only be the readiness to let go of all. Let go doubt, let go fear, let go guilt. There are conditions: "Abandon fear all ye who enter here." Abandon guilt, abandon time. You are moving out of time, you are moving through the gateway into the eternal that is outside the time scale, into ethereal space.

I feel around me the beings who would strive to hold me back. These are the darker angels who would bind the soul to past regrets and future fears. But their backward, downward drag is weakened and eliminated by the radiation of the light. I move forward. It burns out the negative. I feel the blast around my temples, into my throat, into my heart, through my limbs. Of course this is a kind of death, death into life. I am in the group of us who have been taken and are now gathered around the central source of light, a central column which is lighter than light, warmer than warmth. It is a presence, a being, it is asking a question, it is playing on our consciousness: "What have you done for me? What are you prepared to do for me? Will you leave all and follow me? I want you. You are of me. You are mine. But there is total freedom. You may leave still, before the door shuts". Nothing, Lord, will take me from this. I want you, total You. I let go everything that I am, that I was. I give all that I am and will be. It is for this that I came. This is the gateway. This is the way through. I ask that I may keep this quality of light while I am still bound to a body.

I hear music. There is sounding. A humming that works in my head. The star in the brow begins to glow. There are hands which are fixing also a golden torque over the throat centre. The cross on the heart, in the heart, glows, radiates. Now the power is right down into the feet. Life into the feet. I experience the true feet, the archetype of the foot. I am being given the archetype of the human body, the body into which I am to develop.

I feel, I look down in thought into the feet. I see the articulated bones, I see the beauty of the arches. Consciousness moves up to the head. I *am* the head. The globe of the head is floating there. My consciousness is both in and around it, looking at it. For around my body is a great cloud of light. I *am* the cloud of light. And it is forming into the vortex of the head. I see the eyes from behind, from inside and I consciously look through them. I can play the beam of the eye in any direction. That which it touches is revealed in its essence. I look out into the forest and the eye-beam reveals the glowing life in the trees. It reveals the life and light, the one light, the divine life.

I know the eye to be an organ of the sun. It is a wound burned into the head which crystallises into the eye organ through which I, the Self, can look. This ethereal eye sees the light in every form, that is the Idea, the being, in every form. Sense of sight, sense of hearing, another break in to the globe of the head. I experience the growth, the development of the skeleton, out of the head. First a fluid vaporous form, a light form. I feel the shaft that is to be the spine, a focal point of tremendous strength, the stream, the column. The great cage of the ribs, holding the heart and I am a light body, a life structure in which there can be no disease. I am allowed forward to be embraced by the Master, to be blessed by the column, the central flow of light energy and of love. I am allowed to kneel, for this is overwhelming. Into the beating heart is planted a power of love. Into the limbs, strength and beauty, into the head, light and thought. Let me be worthy of receiving the Christ light. I claim my light. I claim my Christ-hood. Strike, strike down. Everything can be burnt out. I am yours. I belong to Christ, the Lord. Help me to make that good. Help me to live out my time, filled with this love, this courage, this light, this total forgiveness. Forgive me Lord as I forgive those who trespass against me. Deliver me from the evil. Hallowed be Thy name. Thy kingdom come on earth as it is in heaven.

The spaceship is moving. The doors are closed. We turn to look out. The light is behind us and through us, everywhere. There is a sounding, a humming. We rise musically. We move up the scale with lovely chords, the earth falls beneath us. We watch the earth reduce in size. We are falling upwards, expanding, lifting, floating. We approach up to the mother ship. It is as if this is the underside of a cloud of ethereal substance, the outer crust of another realm. Many ships are docking under this, for it is a huge area. It is really a surround of the earth, which is small below us. We are being released to walk out, to walk up, to walk through.

We walk out in our warmth bodies. There is no weight, no gravity. We move where we direct our attention. I take hands with my companion, my guide. I feel the love surrounding. I remain an individuality, but here I experience the blending. Try it, we can move through each other. Try it. We are floating over a lake, with wonderful forests. And I am being shown the mountains. I and my guide, and there are others with us, are drawn up a mountain valley. There is forming in the plateau in the high valley, a little town, yes it has walls, shining walls, and gates. The gate is thrown open for us to enter. We move by thought, we are where we direct attention, but I keep with my guide. Up the steps of the temple.

Angelic Guide speaking:

You have been watching with your imagination. This gives you some sense of the scope and scale of things, for infinite variety. You see what it means to be lifted into the mother ship. Of course that can happen, of course that will happen to those who are prepared. You have moved out of time as you understand it. You have spent a short time, half an hour of your earth time and will shortly click back again, but you experience the two-fold consciousness, your own earth-bound consciousness and the great fact of the Oneness of all being and Identity with the Oneness.

That which you form with your imagination is real; how can it be other? There is this city, this temple, this mountain, these lakes, these forests. You and your little group are surrounded now by the cloud of light. We move in the light. Wisdom lives in the light. Now I ask you to look down from this height. You are looking from an angelic level. You are experiencing the wonder of our plane, but look down to Earth.

Experience with me now, take my hand, let me blend with you. I'm taking you down again. Zoom down to Earth. Let the Earth enlarge. Plunge into the earth atmosphere. Keep the cocoon of light round you. We are simply lowering, coming down the frequency bands, plunging into earth atmosphere. Come down and find your own waiting body. Approach it from above. Surround it with the light. You are not your body, but you may bless it. It is a frail thing. Pour your light into it. Pour your strength into it. You are a Christed being who is now going to operate for the day in a body. You are going to hold the light of the cloud, in mind and in heart, the love and the sense of Oneness. You are one in heart with them all. See the cocoon of light, cloud of light surrounding your aura. You now bring down into your physical body and into the cleansed emotional body, some recollection of the light where you've been. Is this not like the near-death experience? You are waking up. You are becoming alive. You have experienced that you are part of the unitary body of humanity. All of you are fibres in the one body of love.

You are going to spend the day now on the earth plane walking with Christ. I hold your hand, I am there. I shall stay with you. Let my thinking be your thinking. As we impinge upon the events of the day, know that I will put the thoughts in your mind. You are now striving to live moment to moment—in the NOW.

There isn't any past. There isn't any future. Fear of the future, remorse about the past are expunged. This is the forgiveness of the Christ, He that is the Lord of Karma. The soul is virgin again.

But now you are going to move through the day. You will come back into time. You'll now know what the descent of the UFO means. Back into the little ship, back down to Earth, back into the earth forest, and the doors are thrown open. You are now the radiant light being who can walk out into a physical body. The physical body is itself like a tiny UFO. You have to have a body of some sort. The body is a focal point. You've called it the temple, which enables you to work now in the density of gravity. Walk lightly, poised between the world of gravity and the realm of levity. Earth is a spaceship. The body is a temple. The UFO is simply a temple, a spaceship, a structure, a body, that can carry "being" between frequencies. You've been expanded up into the mother ship which you have discovered to be the Whole, the great Oneness, in which everything is. Now you have come back again and taken over your body, but it is cleansed, Christed, full of light, full of love. It can hurt no-one. Now I'll hand you back to yourself. Do not doubt. You move from dullness, through doubt into integrity of thought, blessedness of soul.

Be blessed. I am with you always.

The Validity of Channelling

THERE IS AN intimate and inner relation between a higher world of living thought and being, and its expression in the realm of physical appearance. We are 'alive' now, in the visible, tangible world. We live in a body in which intelligence and intellect can manifest, using the five senses for experience and interpretation. With the overdevelopment of the left hemisphere of the brain and its intellectual faculties in the last few centuries, we have clearly lost much of the faculties of the right brain, the more sensitive, poetic, visionary powers that can apprehend the supersensible worlds.

We have established beyond doubt that the Higher Worlds are a reality and that they can be explored. Indeed this is one of the great adventures of our age. Furthermore, in the light of global changes indicated from the turn of the century, the bridge of contact will become vitally important. Channelling is a bridging between our normal consciousness and the 'higher worlds'. The fact that this field can be open to deception and misunderstanding does not mean that it is invalid to work for this inner contact between the planes of being. Indeed, it must be achieved.

Channelling has had an interesting history over the last century. In the late 19th century mediumship held interest for many, chiefly in the attempt to make contact with those who had 'passed on'. Here the primary motive was to establish and prove survival of death. Great names were associated, including Sir Oliver Lodge. The seances most certainly produced some interesting phenomena, but it must be recognized that these sessions involved a lowering of consciousness in the medium—which could lead to illness and breakdown.

In direct contrast is the achieving of knowledge of the higher worlds through intensifying of thinking. This was the achievement of Rudolf Steiner, whose contribution is of profound significance. Born in 1864 with a first rate scientific intellect, he found that he possessed complete inner vision of the spiritual worlds. He soon found that his fellow students could not see what was open to him—the reality of spiritual beings working everywhere, throughout the natural kingdom. But he recognized that this was a strange throw-back to an older form of knowledge, not consonant with the scientific intellect of the age. He therefore decided never to speak about his spiritual vision until he had so intensified his thinking that he could recover this knowledge as genuine scientific investigation of the invisible worlds with fully conscious thinking. He had to make it quite clear that his spiritual knowledge was *not* mediumship, but an achievement of intensified thinking. Therefore he warned his followers against what was then understood as channelling.

When at the turn of the century Steiner launched into spiritual teaching, he demonstrated an unlimited possibility of spiritual knowledge and its application to all aspects of living. It was of course vital to him that no-one should think that his complete width of knowledge of the higher worlds was achieved through 'mediumship'. He had achieved a true intensifying of thinking to explore higher knowledge and to merge thinking with the consciousness of beings on the spiritual planes.

This momentous achievement of Steiner's is of profound relevance to our broad picture of channelling. It truly indicates the emergence of a new type of human being, one who has taken a deliberate step in consciously lifting and intensifying thinking, so that his mind can blend with Mind and Being in the spiritual world.

Our picture must be that the human entity, the I AM in each of us, is a droplet of divinity, immortal and therefore axiomatically imperishable, belonging to the higher worlds of spirit, but dipping into embodiment for training and experience on Planet Earth, the greatest school for souls. Upon Earth the human race experiences freedom of choice. We may therefore be led astray by the 'adversary forces'—the tempters who inflate egoism and deny the spirit. We need many lives on earth in order to go through the long training and ultimately to transform our soul and mind so that we may, in freedom, become co-creators with God.

Now it becomes clear that bridging between the material and spiritual planes is vitally important. We are called on in this age to develop consciousness that can rightly channel information and make direct contact with discarnate beings within our own conscious thinking. This obviously has its dangers, since there are many evil beings who would strive to take possession of human souls. In the great school of Earth we are learning to master our own souls and ultimately reach the point when we can truly allow ourselves to be flooded with all-embracing Love—which in truth is the power of the living Cosmic Christ. It has been said that Earth, created as the Planet of Wisdom, is now to be transformed into the planet of Love. This is the true meaning of the Second Coming and it is taking place in our generation as we approach the millenium.

The world is now ready for a dissolving of barriers between the planes of matter and spirit. Therefore, with a new validity, direct channelling emerges and is a vital factor in the spiritual awakening of our time. It is an essential exploration. Like the explorers of the first Elizabethan Age, we must recognize the dangers inherent in our exploration, while launching out into the adventure of blending in consciousness with higher worlds.

On the higher planes of being we are, as spiritual entities, instantly wherever we project our attention. And where love exists between two beings, we may be sure that the 'other one' is instantly there, blending mind and heart when we send out our thought and call. Once attuned, we may indeed talk mentally with them. A vista of possibilities open as this inner converse is mastered and used. This is a bridging operation of wonder and beauty and we are called on to cultivate this inner channelling so that we may move with courage and certainty into and through an era of change.

We now grasp the immense importance and validity of the true channelling—the cultivation of the ability to allow the thoughts and teachings of higher Mind to enter our human minds. It opens a vast field which can include the heights of wisdom, but also the deception of lesser beings whose motives may be dangerous seduction and the denial of the Spirit.

The basic truth is that the being from the Higher World speaks to us *from within our own thinking*. Mind blends with mind. It may appear that we have merely thought or spoken our own thoughts. Then sometimes we may know with absolute certainty that we are thinking or speaking as a channel for a being out of the body. When a dear friend 'dies' we may at first feel that he or she is lost to us. Then we realize that, freed from the body, they are very close, drawn by the bond of love. They are where we are, but blended heart to heart and mind to mind. This can become the most beautiful relationship. Of course it is most important to overcome the unreasoning grief which will drag the departing soul down and hamper its progress. We must release it into the light and send it forth on its journey with courage and hope. And then, by loving thought, allow it to blend with our own soul when occasion arises or the call is sent out from either side.

There may be the doubt that this is simply 'me talking to me'. But we must 'test the spirits' through the quality of the channelling. Obviously the process varies with everyone. With some who are highly sensitive, it becomes a real inner conversation or dictation. Read for instance the wonderful new book by Ken Carey called *Starseed: The Third Millenium*. Ken describes how he was truly taken over in fullest consciousness, and the book was dictated to him, chapter by chapter. This is an example of channelling at its most wonderful and advanced. Clearly such contact is of immense significance for the coming time.

We have in the last century so over-developed the intellectual faculties of the left-brain reasoning, that right-brain intuition has too often fallen into disuse and become dormant. Yet the wonder is that MIND (in God) is directly in touch with 'mind' in the human being. Knowledge or inspiration can be given in the instant intuitive flash from Higher Mind. The intellectual left hemisphere will demand reason and will doubt and question and analyse. The faculty of intuitive mind-response has in the Age of Reason been too often left unused. Yet it holds the most marvellous secrets and guards the portal of vision.

Blake as visionary wrote:

> *Now I will a fourfold vision see*
> *And a fourfold vision is given to me*
> *Fourfold is my supreme delight*
> *And threefold in soft Beulah's night*
> *And twofold always. May God us keep*
> *From single vision and Newton's sleep.*

'Single vision' represented for him the reliance on left hemisphere intellect at the price of atrophying of the organ of direct spiritual perception operating through the right hemisphere with its direct inner vision. Blake takes 'Newton' as symbol for the high development of intellectual thinking, which, while being essential, may preclude spiritual vision and contact.

So, in our so-called 'New Age thinking', we take part in a general awakening of a mental activity in direct contact with spiritual and super-sensible Mind. The result is a very wide flow of channelled knowledge. How often we hear people say "My guidance told me. . ." or "I was given such and such information." A whole vista of new potential is opening up, which basically implies that right-hemisphere mind is allowing the more sensitive, poetic faculties, so long dormant in our very intellectual culture, to become operative as direct channels for spiritual thinking and apprehension. Thus the New Age is characterized by channelling as a central feature of the present awakening. Of course it is at times simple, since it represents the awakening of largely dormant faculties. But in our time the direct contact becomes a phenomenon of immense potential and importance. Perhaps it is behind the remarkable melting of barriers in our western culture, so notable in the last few years, and symbolized by the coming down of the Berlin Wall.

Let us have the courage to accept channelling as a major factor in the spiritual awakening of our time. It represents the dissolving of frontiers and a true recognition that humankind is One and that every soul is a droplet of divinity, immortal, imperishable, and interlinked. And let us recognize that marvellous channelling of highest quality is now in full flood, bringing vision, courage, confidence and joy.

The wonderful volumes of spiritual teaching by the Arcane School come from direct channelling of the Master K.H. by Alice Bailey. A stream of books based on direct right-hemisphere contact is now flooding the alternative bookshops. At its finest, channelling of spiritual knowledge through sensitive souls who can listen to the inner voice of their higher guides or link with friends 'out of the body', is a major factor in the redemption of mankind through the rising tide of Love.

Planet Earth is to be cleansed of its greed and violence through humanity opening to the divine Love impulse, which *is* the real Second Coming in our time. And channelling is an essential vehicle for this "Operation Redemption". While we remain wise to the dangers of too superficial contact with the higher worlds, let us accept the present flood of channelling as a primal factor in the redemption of benighted humanity.

Coming Home

THE I AM speaks, Christ-filled:

Yes, you are coming home.

Home is where I AM.

You have shut yourself off. You, all of you, over the last centuries, have built your castles of defence, your strong, stone walls, your battlements, your moats.

You have felt the need to protect yourselves.

You have been motivated by fear and all that comes from fear—all the evil beings of criticism and hate, doubt, dislike and disappointment. Your city has been occupied by these enemy forces. You have been enslaved in serving them. You have thought it necessary to build this strong fortress with its flinty front and façade.

Now I AM calling on you to dissolve the barriers, slight the castle, destroy all defences, knowing that, receiving ME, you have the perfect and only defence. Draw around your consciousness the cloud of golden light, alive, comforting, warm. You are surrounded by this golden glow.

Lift, lift out of the hard stone. See it becoming translucent.

As you rise to My frequency, the stone appears to melt, to fade, finally to disappear. Like your old Cotswold stone walls, it finally disintegrates and returns to soil. See the site of the castle now, a mound in which archaeologists can dig for foundations. Now you are centred in the golden cloud. The core, the kernel, glows and shines. Within the mind, within the heart, is light.

So simply you are come home. You drive out the spirits of darkness, those negative emotions. You throw away all the old weapons of defence of the ego based on fear.

You cut out from your vocabulary all words of doubt, despair, discouragement, dislike, distaste, distress, desperation, disappointment. This is the dark city of Dis. Before your mouth a threshold be guarded. Let no words today come through your lips motivated by these dark beings of negativity. Put them all aside. They have no place in the golden cloud. So long as you sustain the light-filled sphere, they cannot enter. The two cannot live together. If you let the dark in, the golden light of My presence will withdraw and fade. This is the one thing you can hold to. You have dissolved the bastions and fortifications. They are dead mounds now. You are floating above them. You are the lighted cloud with its shining star centre, My centre. Cut out the spoken words. Cut out the thoughts which those words express. Thought is so quick. You must therefore learn to watch your thought like a fencer. You once handled the foils so beautifully. What a symbol! Watch to parry any attack. Touché! A touch a touch, I do confess!

Remember that whenever you consciously create the cloud and throw down those defences, you become vulnerable, like a new born creature. This is both a coming home and a birth into a new tenderness, a tender and gentle creature. Therefore My defence, the Christ Power, is absolutely vital and while I AM there it gives you total protection, for any missile of dark thought, any projectile shot at the soul, will be deflected and dissolved and rejected. It cannot live in the Light. Therefore watch the thoughts. They are also the vocabulary, even if unspoken. They can be daggers to stab other souls. Therefore have you built your fortress defences, built because of fear, not love. At last, after so long, you are coming through, coming home, building your true interior temple in the NOW. It is the living Now, this ever moving flowing moment, continuously in touch with Me, the Christ and your angels. You have the unit of this day to play with, work with. Move through it. Enjoy it. Forgive yourself all that is past, as you are forgiven. Love Me wherever you see Me, in human, animal, bird, plant, angel. Submit, surrender, dissolve all protection, but take Me, the power of the Living Christ.

So be it.

I Want one Thing

I AM ONCE MORE outside the great bastion wall and gate, through which I could not make entry. There was darkness and weight in my embodiment which debarred the crossing of the threshold. Now I stand in my surrounding cloud of light, my local defensive field around my aura. But now I am joined by one that I love. We blend; we unite. Love is activated between us. I bring to the threshold the love of another human being. In commitment I step forward offering myself for entry. I move further into the shining of the light, the great rays of light which penetrate my whole being. The light again fills the crown chakra, spreads into Head, shines from the brow, down to the throat, down to the Heart. Let it begin to glow. Down to solar plexus, the sun centre, and continue down with its cleansing action into the darker will area, the sacral centre, the ajna centre and on into the limbs.

There is a burning-out of ego desire. I am committed to taking the choices that make for Wholeness, WHATEVER is involved. To the best of my ability, I reject the ego desires. My intention, when faced with choice, is to choose always that course that makes for greater wholeness, to make the world more whole, to join consciously with this evolutionary drive towards wholeness, whatever that involves.

That is my wish as from now. When I choose wrongly, you, my guides, will quickly make it clear and give me another opportunity to try again. When I freely choose aright, then you will flood your energy and light through me and I shall know that the course is the right one.

It often matters very little which course is chosen. What matters is to *make* the choice and act into it, watching above all for that intuitive flash which almost always comes *first* at the moment of choice and is so often overlaid by the interference of rational intellect. I am training myself to move into new situations under your guidance, dedicated and rededicated to following the path of wholeness. This is holism in action. More and more human beings will take this course.

The morphogenic field of humanity is being activated by every one of the race who adopts this course. It is the endless adventure. I repeat that what matters is cultivating the ability to take the conscious choices, preferring always to take the bolder, more difficult, more exciting course rather than the more timid one which seems to satisfy personal desire.

I choose the course of Wholeness, *whatever* it involves, however much the 'ego-desires', react against it. This will help in the burning out of self. I submit this and, blended in love with another soul, I stand directly in the beam of light.

Acceptance I know and now we are drawn through the Gate into the Light.

A throng of beings receive us. My little cloud-aura is enlarged and strengthened by the blending with others I love and who love me. It is therefore intensified, for they also become part of my thinking. They live in my thinking, which now bears and carries spiritual beings. I act in the certainty that my beloved friends are using my thinking. What I think is them. To this concept I respond, in action.

We now move up to the Square, the cathedral ahead of us. Sufficient for now that we have made entry. When I look at those accepted I can see the glowing point in the forehead and the light of the heart—passport to eternity.

I can, with ease, come back to the Square for further exploration. So we leave it now.

(The inspiration for this section comes from the delightful book *I Want One Thing*, by Frances Horn.)

The Crystal Sphere— your Original Face

You HAVE ENTERED the Light and the Life. Hold it in perfect stillness and serenity. You know by direct experience that the darker emotions, moods and beings are repelled by the Light. For them it is intolerable. They may assault your interior castle, but they cannot conquer it—unless you surrender and give them entry.

You are peering through a crystal sphere of sight and vision. You experience this wonderful evolution of an organ of thought and sense which can behold the wholeness of life. But you have been entirely unaware of the marvel of sheer design which makes this possible.

Look out from your crystal sphere. Have now the simplicity of childhood and hold critical intellect at bay. "Except ye become as little children. . ." What is this so-called face? Now go gently and stay simple. You know about your face through looking in a mirror. You have intellectually grasped the concept of the retina of the eye receiving images and reversing them. You have seen diagrams of the amazing mechanism of the ear. But unless these organs are ill and you have ear-ache or eye-ache or headache you are totally unaware of them. In actual experience, if you are childlike, honest and simple, your face becomes like one shining eye, an open crystal sphere, through which you look out. Through it you see your clothes, your feet, the bookcase, the window, and beyond it the trees and houses.

They are all in this crystal sphere. So are the clouds and the stars. Where does it end?

It was *Douglas Harding* who first was hit by this concept—'I haven't got a face'. As a student of Zen he understood why the Zen masters would say "cut off your head" and then roar with laughter. They called the crystal sphere your 'original face' in which you could perceive all that is.

Harding wrote an enchanting and challenging little book *On having no Head*, and he saw his teaching as a kind of western Zen.

In your real experience, everyone else you see has this remarkable 8 inch lump on their shoulders, pierced with seven holes and with hair on top—but not you! You are, in your experience, unique in possessing the crystal sphere, and for each one of them the experience is the same. Each person is unique in carrying this amazing organ of perception, in which the universe is contained. For, be honest—where does your original face stop?

Traherne writes in his *Centuries of Meditations*:

> You will never enjoy the world aright till the sea floweth in your veins, till you are clothed with the heavens and crowned with the stars, and perceive yourself to be the sole heir of the whole world, and more than so because men are in it who are every one sole heir as well as you.

It needs the simplicity of a little child to see this great truth. Drop all 'face-saving', all 'putting a bold face on things', and 'facing up to things'. Throw away your face and accept the crystal sphere which contains all things on which it directs its attention. I take away your face and give you the universe! Like a little child you can enter the Kingdom.

The design, the sheer artistry of this creation, is far beyond our understanding and we take it for granted! There is *design* behind all evolution. Within nature has been produced a being with a nervous system and a brain through which matter can be lifted into consciousness. The Divine field has evolved the human being, as a culminating point in nature, because the universe needs this organ 'in the likeness of God' within the field of matter. The human being is that point where nature can become conscious of itself and reflect the living Ideas in the Mind of God and so become creative in freedom.

It is indeed possible for the angelic beings to enter into human consciousness and look out of the human eye in order to see what the work of creation looks like from within. As we reach this point in evolution they can blend with us in thought and experience their creation, while we can begin to break out of limitation and separation, and identify with the Unitary Being of Humanity, designed after the image of God.

As we reach this point, the beings of the lighter worlds can blend with us in thought, while we can learn to look and listen with a greater refinement, because our consciousness is merged with theirs. The angels then can look at the forms of nature through our eyes, while we can look with the eye of the mind at the being and life within the forms. This is the great step in exploration into God, for God IS the life in all things.

Green Man Experience

I come directly into the Garden.
I float as a point of consciousness and light and
   thought and vision.
I project myself and am accepted and drawn through the
   door out of the darkness into the Light. Into the green.
I become the Green Man, the head which is one with the
   fronds of green plants.
Whatever I touch, I am.
I am the green in the grass.
I am the life in the ferns.
I directly blend with the elemental being
   within the ferns,
   within the daffodils,
   within the bulb under the Earth.
I am within the green shoot,

the first tiny tree which is to become the great beech.

I am outside Time, before time.

Before the beech tree was, I AM.

Vast floating bonded by nothing.

No matter, body, sense, gravity, nor any bond bonding.

I am the vast being of the Imagination

I am out of my body.

I can look down and see my body, knowing that I can
come back.

This is just like the near-death experience.

I have lifted clear of the body,

I have been drawn into the light, which is, of course,
a great Presence.

For I experience indeed that the Christ Power is
everywhere, in everything.

I do not need to see Him as a visible being.

He is the light. He is the being within
every form.

What was without now works within.

I am one with it, with Him.

This is so beautiful and so simple.

Death is a birth. This is the equivalent of having
died. I am now one with all life—

Kinship with all life.

There is nothing I cannot love.

Love is the recognition of the Divinity within each thing,

The same Divinity as is in me.

I am instantly where I project consciousness—

On to the top of the Mountain

Into the Temple—temple of Time, Gateway of Eternity.

I am out into the blue of Eternity.

I am in Time anywhere.

I am back in Time or forward into future.

I shall be able to see what it was like.

I look right back into the molten world
seething, foaming, changing, forming, hardening.

I look forward and on in time.
Passing over the present moment of manifestation.
I see again a changing world,
Rushing of waters.
Movement of the structure, shredding,
    lifting, breaking, new mountains rising.
I see humanity then as a field of light,
    surrounding the Earth.
Those souls lifted out of their bodies
    become a cloud of light or strands of darkness,
Which are drawn out and form a darker planet.
They pull out through release from embodiment.
Clouds of darkness composed of soul quality
    coagulate and are drawn away
And form into an unlighted planet,
Which begins to solidify again,
That the souls may be given the opportunity of rebirth.
And I see how on our planet,
    surrounded by the fair luminous cloud
    enveloping the Earth,
These light-filled souls, one with all the archetypal
    beings, can then begin with consciousness
To form and build a New World.
The Earth is alight.
The Earth has given birth to consciousness.
All those who are beyond self
    and into the Oneness are shining a light.
Therefore the whole planet is surrounded
    by Light. Glory be!
O God how wonderful!
All the souls who before have achieved
    the conquest of ego and the entry to
    the heart of love,
They all join together
Innumerable angelic light beings,
    winged beings.

Sorrow and pain are transmuted into beauty.
Agony, remorse, regret—forgiveness lifts
these. The pain of all that individual souls
have gone through in the struggle of embodiment,
this is turned into a new beauty.
"These things shall be: a loftier race
Than e'er the world has known shall rise
With fire of freedom in their hearts
And light of knowledge in their eyes."

So be it.

Sacred Sympathy

I ENTER THE GARDEN. I am disembodied. I am a point of floating consciousness. So are you, my Guide. We meet as beings of thought. You speak in my thinking. There is at once a blending, and with it immediately is created a responsibility to sustain this blending of thought. I obviously must exercise all sympathy, tolerance, love. Otherwise the blending would be unmaintainable, intolerable, and even give opportunity for dark attack.

As you, Genesis, can slide into me with such gentle ease, so I enter the company, the soul group, for many other beings are living in your thinking. It is a Christed group held together by mutual attunement and love. If I came with irritation, criticism, hate, worry, cynicism, negative emotion, it would bring an intolerable irritant into the group and I should be rejected. These are the terms on which I may stay in the garden.

This is not sentiment. It is a simple fact that a subtle relationship remains impossible, unsustainable, without serenity and sacred sympathy. Thus once in the Garden I am surrounded by the structure or Cloud of Light. Genesis, you now speak to me.

Genesis speaking:

> Listen George, what you have been speaking is already Me. You are grasping the concept and the experience of blended thinking. You have realised that fallen humanity puts itself out of the Garden into the darkness. If you feed on criticism, fear and hate, you exclude yourself from our light. Entirely your own choice. Consciousness is blending. There are indeed other beings who are not of our light, who are only too happy to step

into your thinking. You perpetually exclude yourselves from what you call the Garden. You simply have no entry so long as the darker side of the ego is operative.

Can you see how important forgiveness is? Forgiveness and love are two sides of the same coin. That does not mean lack of discrimination. It does mean Sacred Sympathy, an understanding of motives and reasons for people's actions and characters. Now you can see that human society is being infiltrated, in the best sense of the word, by a force which is the emergence of a new humanity. Look into that great ocean of Christ consciousness. Beings innumerable, blended in heart and thought, light and love, sympathy, tolerance and forgiveness. You and yours are actively in the field of battle. That is what incarnation implies. Your souls have taken on this task of being the bridging point, the fringe force. The risk, of course, is that you in free choice are allowed to let ego dominate. Inevitably, when desire, fear, criticism and dislike become dominant, you then fall to a lower frequency that cuts you out from the light. Then you are possessed by beings of darkness. You are dragged down into the gravity field.

So-called 'possession' can be a terrible condition, when a lost soul or dark being actually gets into a personality. But realise that a condition of cynicism, fear and dislike, and its expression in thought and emotion, is a blending of being. Just as you are blending being with me within your thinking and your heart, all the time you are blended with much wider groupings of spirit., Having chosen to enter the Garden, then you begin a great exploration, but the terms for allowing you to stay are that you watch yourself and cut out from your heart and thought all ego desires, all the lower, frightened, angry, disappointed self. You have been touched by certain disappointments. You must fight this. No one else can. Have the courage to see that 'whatever is, is right'. Sometimes a difficult doctrine, but absolutely fundamental. Start from where you are, in my presence.

Blessings upon you.

All nature is but art, unknown to thee,
All chance, direction which thou canst not see,
All discord, harmony not understood,
All partial evil, universal good,
And, spite of pride, in erring reason's spite
One truth is clear—Whatever IS, is RIGHT.

(Alexander Pope)

Affirmations and the Life Energy

I CREATE IN Imagination the luminous cloud enveloping my body and aura, impregnating me with warmth and light. I call upon you, Genesis, my Guide and Teacher, and you have given me the assurance that when I do so you are there. This implies that the angelic consciousness can be anywhere and everywhere. You are part of that great Oneness of Mind—the Mind of God which is omnipresent. We, in our human separation, had to learn that the divine ocean of love and wisdom is always everywhere. Higher beings will speak and think in you. You can think in me.

The impulse to speak with you is tantamount to your thinking in me—I need this contact.

I must establish a flow with you.

I must get beyond the sense that I alone create my thoughts.

Imagination is the power to lift thinking into the great Oneness of life, beyond the limitations of the sense world. Then we see that the life in everything is the same life, One Life.

Yes, my friend, know that you are always part of the great Oneness but you have related yourself to the separation. Attune now to the Oneness and discover that everything is within yourself. The greater Self includes everything to which you give your attention. You make the whole one Self. Sacred sympathy implies recognizing, with love, the beauty and wonder of life in anything you see. One Life! Identify with the Oneness of creation, for you as a human being are part of God in the Wholeness.

Grapple with your imagination. Perceive all within consciousness. Where does the withinness begin or end? It is like a glove turned inside out, or that Japanese fan folded and then opened to show the expanded circle. Identify with Light and Life. Know that the greater Self is the Oneness of Light with which you now consciously unite. That Self never ends. The exploration is endless and glorious.

Rightly and inevitably you will begin to love the light within every form you meet. In all human idiosyncrasies, in all struggles and imperfections, it is wonderful. Nature is very perfect in its working. The body is part of Nature and it too is very perfect. The astral body, the soul nature of man, is still very imperfect and chaotic. Humanity, in the deeper sense, is that Divine power of thought and light which holds everything in harmony and balance, for it is the power of the spirit playing with joy through form. Often the being has little or no consciousness of this plan. The animal, the insect, the plant, manifest the workings of God's plan, but are not conscious of them. Instinct is the Divine Thinking, the thought of the archetypes or group egoes of the animals, evolved to fulfil necessary action. The human being is the creature into whom the ego can fully descend. In him can be chaos and disturbance and even a complete failure to work to the divine plan.

Now you can see the profound significance of this inner movement within individual humans to take conscious constructive control of themselves. Of course human freedom has resulted in much egoism and desire to satisfy the lust for power and sensation and possession of wealth.

The true human entity exists in the Mind of God. He, the Source, has thought you. Therefore there is no fear that you should be extinguished with the dissolving of the physical body. You are a strand of this whole ocean of thought, which is ubiquitous God. When you move over at so-called death, you will enter a realm where you can experience forests, rivers, men and mountains, and indeed, anything you can imagine. You are taken into a light-filled realm of infinite diversity. It is a condition of consciousness and it is everywhere, beyond time and space. You may assume that your true identity is immortal, for you are a strand of the ocean of consciousness. When your physical body has been dissolved, you are freed as a soul and spirit, and you live now in the others. You are all strands in this ocean of Life that is also Love.

On the higher planes all that you meet are also aspects of you, the greater You, the unified Humanity. You are a cell of that unitary *consciousness. Humanity is still in a pre-birth condition and is approaching the awakening to its totality of being.*

Look back on Earth and see it filled with half-awake creatures, all fighting each other, as beings encapsulated in ego and sense. Experience the ego drive of the lower self with its desires and its denial of the Spirit, possessed by the powers of darkness and the passions of Lucifer. Now behold the change through the totality of your Imagination. Let all human entities realize themselves as aspects of the Whole.

* * * * * *

Here I quote a passage from Coleridge.

> *There is one Mind, one omnipresent Mind*
> *Omnific. His most holy name is Love.*
> *Truth of subliming import . . .*
>   *'Tis the sublime in man,*
> *Our noontide majesty, to know ourselves*
> *Parts & proportions of one wondrous whole.*
> *This fraternises man . . .*
>
>   *Toy bewitched*
> *Made blind by lusts, disinherited of soul*
> *No common centre man, no common sire*
> *Knoweth! A sordid, solitary thing*
> *Mid countless brethren with a lonely heart*
> *Through courts & cities the smooth savage roams*
> *Feeling himself, his own low self, the whole*
> *When he by sacred sympathy might make*
> *The whole one Self! Self that no alien knows*
> *Self, far diffused as fancy's wing can travel*
> *Self, spreading still! Oblivious of its own*
> *Yet all of all possessing! This is Faith!*
> *This the Messiah's destined victory!*

(Samuel Taylor Coleridge)

PART V

Breakthrough

Towards a Chain Reaction

I AM A POINT of spirit in a world of Spirit.
I am a thought in an ocean of Thought, a strand of loving energy in a sea of love divine.
And thus I stand.
What I think, I AM. If I think thoughts of illness, fear, poverty, I shall draw these qualities of being onto myself. If I think accident I become accident prone. If I think disease, I shall attract illness. Inevitably, what you fear you tend to become. These forces of negativity are beings and they respond when called. Since the human being is designed as a structure for embodying the spirit and has been given free choice, he can build into himself the tendencies he chooses. This seems inevitable. "Ask and ye shall receive." It all turns on what you choose to ask. It is your choice. If you think courage and joy, these qualities will be drawn to you.

God is the Life in everything, everywhere.
The amazing thought is therefore that the Creator, the I AM, the Source, is immediately present everywhere all the time. I however, have to take the initiative to make contact and open to this universal power and being. It's no use my simply telling an electric light to go on. I have to take the initiative and switch on. Then light and power instantly flow from the great source.

It should clearly be possible to keep in touch and switched on to God all the time. It is called the Practice of the Presence of God. The mystics and holy ones have achieved it and we are all free to follow. This is the major task for a human being, the purpose of our incarnation—to attune consciously to the flow of God power. It may take a lifetime to achieve the step. No matter. We have the whole of eternity to work this one out. It is for this that we incarnated on Earth.

Now, meditate on the living Earth. See her turning in space, a living, thinking, sensitive creature. See the film of life around her, those myriad points of divine humanity, those sparks of God-fire housed in the temple structure we call a body. See how so many are filled with fear and anger and violent emotion, and see the result that the delicate web of life in nature is being rent and torn, and is withering and dying. Try to conceive and feel the vast sea of pain pouring forth from this suffering planet.

Then conceive THE EVENT. Use Imagination. An impulse flows through human consciousness. One God-droplet after another pauses, ceases to react to fear, hate and violence, and instead calls on God and his Angels of Light. What happens? Instantly that tiny centre begins to glow luminous. This is infectious and begins to spread. If disease is infectious, why not the positive 'Ease'—the joy, love, courage syndrome. Here surely is the most superb example of Rupert Sheldrake's morphogenic field in action. Do it first in imagination. Let us all look down upon the turning, stricken planet and see the lighting-up begin. It leaps from point to point. The whole surrounding cloud of consciousness becomes luminous and glows. The impetus, tentative at first and starting from separated pin points of light consciousness, coheres into an ever widening field.

Where there is light, the darkness is driven back. The stronger the light the darker the shadows: the shadows represent powers of evil and negativity, hate and fear, despair and greed, and all the terrible emotions. These beings of evil (for such they are) have no compunction about direct attack to take possession of human beings. Yet we know that Light and Love, which work for human freedom, will not take over until invoked. They are infinitely stronger when given free entry into the human soul.

Thus look again at our planet. The moment is approaching

when a sufficient number of human units will have opened themselves to the light for a chain reaction to begin. Conceive this event. Our infectious 'ease' leaps from one to the next. And the moment approaches when the Earth will burst into flame— the flame of Love, the fire of Michael, the glory of God.

This is an absolute possibility. This is our deed today. We are told that if fifty million people will simultaneously think and pray Peace for an hour in meditative stillness, then it will suffice to start such a chain reaction, such 'morphogenic resonance'. We all recognize that we approach the threshold of entry to the Aquarian Age. A cleansing of the planet must take place. Let us be on this particular band wagon!

Choose to be part of the flooding of the Light and Fire of the Christ. This is the key point we *must* see—that, since we are given freedom, the beings of Light will not take over the human soul unless invoked. The initative is ours. They must remain silent till we call on them, dedicate our lives, submit to the inflow of the light and power of Him whose service is perfect freedom. This is the deed we are called on to do today.

Fire over the Earth

I DRAW AROUND MYSELF the cloak of light, the cloud of light penetrating every cell and fibre of my body. I am lightness. I leave the physical body on the marble seat, and I float out.

I lift in buoyancy and expansion out beyond the tree into its magnetic field, expanding upward, out beyond the atmosphere of the Earth. I am out in orbit, I am in direct touch with my bodily self as the astronaut is in touch with base. Instant oscillation between base and expanded self.

Around me I strengthen the luminous cloud. I am the focal point of light within this protective cloud. Nothing of the dark can remain within the cloud. It is rejected and repelled. Nothing of the negative can enter. It is diverted. Great stillness and serenity fill me. Other beings are drawn in who are attuned. For them there is attraction. That lighted cloud rises as angelic entities, freed souls of love and light, enter and blend.

Our thinking can carry and bear spiritual beings. We *are* one. What I feel to be *my* thinking expands to take into itself the thinking of kindred beings. I totally surrender lower self to become one with a greater, living light-filled Self. The cloud is spinning, sounding, like one of those musical tops. I look down upon the turning Earth. I look out at the galaxy, our luminous spinning cloud *is* a tiny star, a focal point of light-filled being.

I look at Spaceship Earth carrying its cargo of life. But it is dark. Our star is a spaceship. What is a spaceship other than a focal point of intense light into which weightless souls and spirits can be drawn, allowed in if they are attuned, repelled if they are not attuned. The passport for entry is the light in the brow of the soul which has rejected anger, hate, criticism, cynicism, egoism. The cloud expands and strengthens. It is a matrix attracting and drawing in those who have achieved sacred sympathy.

Entry implies that those negative qualities are burnt out. The incandescent light is intolerable to them. They are instantly consumed as by fire. For those souls drawn in, this is a kind of birth. Around the darkened Earth are appearing many focal points of light, little stars. How like the concept of a fleet of spaceships, hovering, forming, capable of expanding and lifting simply by the direction of thought. Exalted thought beings descend, to enter and command the fleet. We who have risen, freed from lower self, accepting the birth into tranquillity, serenity, tolerance, gratitude, joy, inability to hurt, have entry and experience ourselves as part of a greater Self.

Our thinking blends with the higher thinking. If we revert to the ego qualities of criticism, fear, guilt, the time-ridden anxieties, we are thrown out, with the result that instantly the fleet of these star ships disappears from our vision. We would then simply fall back through empty space to the dark physical Earth. But check that fall, lift again, to the frequency at which the ships reappear, giving us entry once more. We see that all the stars are truly focal points of being. Each is a kingdom of beings, visible only to the risen thinking, the living, loving, light-filled thinking.

Humankind is awakening. A birth is taking place. We rediscover the polarity of the matter-bound, sense-bound, death-bound self and the lifted, light-filled, living Self, the greater Self, of which we are truly a cell. This imagination gives us the purpose of man and evolution. We reach the threshold when we can abandon the sleep and nightmare of egoism and float out into the living star. Transmute lower ego. By sacred sympathy make the whole one Self, far diffused as imagination can carry. The only terms are that we reject the qualities of criticism, cynicism, anger, guilt, hate, fear. This is perhaps the meaning of the statement that souls attuned to God and Christ will be lifted out into the spaceships, when real crisis comes.

There are two forms of fire. Look down upon the Earth. There could be the searing explosion of fire consuming life on Earth. There could be that spiritual fire, the burning out, cauterising all that is of the devil of darkness, fear and hate. Look down and look ahead to this lifted consciousness. We can see the dark earth surrounded by innumerable star ships, kindred focal points of light and love, forming into a greater whole, supporting each other, receiving from the heights angelic power that drives out all that is negative and of the soul darkness.

This forms into the fair luminous cloud enveloping the Earth. Our thinking merges with the thinking of greater beings. The gods look down upon the earth and wait their time. This huge fleet of light points forming a great surrounding envelope of light is, of course, quite invisible to physical eyes. The eye of the imagination becomes one with it and can envelop the entire earth. Though this whole picture would disperse immediately when the consciousness reverts to sense-bound thinking, nevertheless it is a far greater strength and durability. This great plane of surrounding light is outside time and physical space. It is the living, unitary being of humanity, a God-being awakened.

The whole purpose of life on Earth is to reach this point of birth and awakening. We are being born into life, and this stupendous realm of spiritual light and life could close in upon the planet. Let that happen. Look forward and see it happen. The whole physical world becomes luminous, a rapid burning out of all soul particles of the evil world, indeed, the counterpart of the atomic nuclear explosion upon Earth. In one instant the Earth could burst into nuclear horror of general explosion. At the same instant, the fire of this stellar world of the living Christ could take over, a force which we have seen repels and throws out all of soul darkness, time-ridden hate and fear. Explosion and counter explosion, a resurrection fire.

Teilhard de Chardin wrote in his "Mass on the World":

> *It is done. Once again Fire had penetrated the earth. . . The flame has lit up the whole world from within. All things individually and collectively are penetrated and flooded by it, from the inmost core of the tiniest atom to the mighty sweep of the most universal laws of being, so naturally has it flooded every element, every energy, every connecting link in the unity of our cosmos, that one might suppose the cosmos to have burst spontaneously into flame.*
>
> *In the new humanity which is begotten today, the Word prolongs the unending act of his own birth and by virtue of his immersion on the world's womb, the great waters of the kingdom of matter have been endued with life.*

What we have seen is the great truth of the coming cleansing of the planet. Let us commit ourselves totally, and in joy, to this great transition and the birth of a new humanity. So be it.

Dynamic Ease

KNOW THIS. Space is filled with an endless ocean of Living Energy. Visible forms and bodies of any sort are coagulations of this energy. The human body is a point through which this energy can be focalized and operative.

Consciousness can direct and handle this. Know also that on the spiritual level you are attuned instantly to the beings to whom you direct attention and thought. Thus your angel guide or your friend out of the body are immediately present when you hold them in mind. Indeed mind blends with mind, a beautiful (or terrible) process. Our great discovery and realisation is that the higher world speaks to us *within our own thinking*. It is not 'out there' but 'in here'. "There is one mind, one omnipresent mind omnific. His most holy name is Love." We are "parts and proportions of one wondrous Whole" (Coleridge). What a responsibility this sets on us! And what an opportunity! This is the meaning of the affirmation "I am with you always, closer than breathing, nearer than hands and feet". What can be closer than breathing other than THINKING?

But now, go further. All life is BEING.

The Living Ideas are truly beings, strands in the vast ocean of the Thought of God outpoured. These are the angels, being of Divine Thought, so alive and operative that they can, at will, take to themselves sheaths enabling them to move into and through planetary densities. Thus beings of exalted light can live on Venus in robes of flame. If we ask "Is there life on Venus", we reply No, because it is too hot. But we are asking the wrong question. We are really asking, "Could this body of mine live on Venus?" Of course it could not. But this does not mean that there is no life on that fiery planet. Its denizens must be so highly evolved on soul and spirit levels that they can take to themselves a body of flame, which you and I could not (yet) do.

Now, all moods, all thoughts, are aspects of this Ocean of Life. Therefore whatever attitude you take, you will draw into yourself corresponding beings. Thus if you choose to think fear and discouragement, anger and criticism, poverty and lack, illness and weakness, lust and greed, dislike and repugnance, these qualities and moods will be drawn into your soul. Blending of minds and moods is the basic manner in which the Living Whole, in its intricate interweaving, works and manifests. Thus you, human being, having freedom to choose your thoughts, are truly a responsible and creative focal point in which, by your own free choice, trends of despair, discouragement, distaste and fear can be actively developed and sent out to add to the darkness in the tapestry of life. If you choose to cut out the negative thoughts and attitudes and to affirm courage, hope, love and joy, you will blend with the corresponding beings and the living, ever changing tapestry will show a spreading point and glowing area of light.

Blending of beings in mind seems to be an absolutely basic principle, and the human being has been given the power of free choice. So, for goodness sake choose light and love, lightness and liberality. How lovely are the messengers that teach us the Gospel of Peace! We must watch our thinking and reacting, for it is *a creative deed*. Because the world is now so dark, dangerous and desperate, we may choose to join the crusade of the Light Bearers. This is not merely an affirmation. It is a recognition of a basic Law of Life. *You are what you think*. You draw to yourself and into yourself and soul the beings who make up the quality you choose to affirm. So for goodness sake cease affirming fear, doubt, and discouragement and ill health. Choose to affirm light, tolerance, tranquillity, prosperity, love and health. This is an active deed. This attitude is infectious and can spread. Choose not to spread the disease of dark moods, but be instrumental in permeating the world with infectious ease. This is to be truly human. Look around you and see that, in all the grim scenario of a modern crumbling society, this active vision of hope and Oneness is spreading. Help it to take hold, like a forest fire, and burn out the dross of dark emotion.

> *For I reckon that the sufferings we now endure bear no comparison with the splendour, as yet unrevealed, which is in store for us. For the created Universe waits with eager expectation for God's sons to be revealed.*
>
> **(Romans 8)**

Batter my Heart
To Christ, our Lord

I THROW AWAY the fortress defences of the self. You can then flood the heart. Intelligence can pour into the thinking. Live this day with me. Drive the evil spirits out of the temple. Drive the money changers out. Drive out all that is fearful, all the guilt. All that is gone. Everything leads up to this point when you, Christ, Master, enter and take over. I give You heart and mind and limb. I will live in this NOW with Your Joy. Guide all my contact with those loving friends who come today and tomorrow.

In place of the fortress defences, build the force-field of light. Let music, movement, light enter this sphere. Let that interior music sound. Your force-field around my aura is total protection. Every evil is thereby dispersed, for how can the evil live within Your light? If it should enter, it would be dissolved. Start from NOW, start from here. Start from me. And let this heart love innumerable others, so that the love of You pours through human hearts. Christ in me. Oh God, Oh Christ, and all my friends around. I need never be lonely again. For You are here. You have given us your word that when we call on You, You are present. Of course You are present, because *You are Life everywhere.* Therefore, the only barrier is what I have built in self-defence; defence of the little self, so that it may go on with its fear and guilt.

On this day I wash out guilt, remorse, regret, fear and ambition. It is for this that this incarnation was given. It is under God's guidance that my life path has been what it has been. The purpose of this incarnation is to surrender absolutely to the power of Christ. This I do. Genesis, be witness, for you are with me here.

I now destroy all self-protective defences and barriers, bastions and battlements. I let you and the force of love and joy take possession in the NOW. There is nothing but NOW, filled with Your love, ever floating, ever moving. You have made, (and we as part of You have evolved), this extraordinary body. I, the real I, am a spiritual being, a star being, a light being. I and my fellows have incarnated, and through this wonderful bodily mechanism can look out and see. We *are* angelic beings looking at the beauty of Nature as a work of art, looking at it from within. If we lose the organ of sight or hearing, we go blind and deaf. We the angelic beings are looking out through a human eye.

As I can blend in consciousness with Genesis, I am giving them the opportunity of looking out from within nature to see the beauty of form, and when I am freed from the body, I shall be directly in touch with the archetypal Ideas which shaped the beauties of nature. My normal seeing cannot apprehend these Ideas, so long as it is sense-bound. But just as the angelic world can enter and see the beauty of nature from within through my eyes, so can I unite with it and, with the eye of the mind, see the creative life and light of this world of idea.

Thus the bridge in experience is achieved. I learn to look with love and perception at every form, to allow the Being within that form to rebound back to me into my heart, that I may go forth with love, through the eye of the mind, to see the Christ within each form. This is the glory. This is the Great Work. It is for this that we came.

I wish to activate the all-seeing Eye of the Mind. Help me. I call on Christ and Genesis to open the All seeing eye that I may apprehend the Being within all form.

Here I quote John Donne's great sonnet:

> Batter my heart, three person'd God; for, you
> As yet but knocke, breathe, shine, and seeke to mend
> That I may rise, and stand, o'erthrow mee, 'and bend
> Your force, to breake, blowe, burn and make me new.
> I, like an usurpt towne, to 'another due,
> Labour to 'admit you, but Oh, to no end,
> Reason your viceroy in mee, mee should defend,
> But is captiv'd, and proves weake or untrue.
> Yet dearely'I love you, 'and would be loved faine,
> But am betroth'd unto your enemie:
> Divorce mee, 'untie, or breake that knot againe,
> Take mee to you, imprison mee, for I
> Except you'enthrall mee, never shall be free,
> Nor ever chast, except you ravish mee.

Twin-souls &
the Binary Relationship

W<small>E ARE GETTING USED</small> to the concept that God lives in everything, wherever Life is apprehended, for HE IS LIFE. The angelic world, itself an aspect of the Living Whole, can blend with the human soul and speaks through it. Your friend out of the body can do the same. We are accepting that this is a bridging between the lower plane of matter and the higher world of spirit into which you are released back at so-called 'death'. Thus what you see, speak, think and feel, could be pure spirit blended with your mortal sense. Of course our bodily make-up will drastically condition the expression of higher being. No matter. We may accept the wonder that this blending is taking place within our thinking and living.

Now I shall attempt to speak about the strangest and most beautiful conception—that of the soul-mate, the twin soul, the binary concept. This is age-old. Plato speaks of it in the "Symposium". Often enough we hear it mentioned. There is a deep longing and hope that we may sometime find our soul-counterpart, and some, with joy, may appear to have achieved it. But we are speaking about something far more than a great love-match or happy marriage. These have of course happened frequently in life, legend and literature. The binary concept is something of vital significance for our present age, when it appears to be re-emerging. It implies that when souls were first formed in ages past, the Divine Plan decreed they should be bifold, male and female in one. Then this primal unity divided and the separated units were launched on their long voyage through time, ever with a deeply implanted desire and longing to find their counterpart or twin and re-unite. That would be the real home-coming.

The binary condition takes on a notably deeper and truer aspect through our spiritual world-view, and thus has only really emerged and begun to be established for our thinking and conceiving in this century. It should be clear that if we lived only one life on Earth there would be little point in talking about soul-twins uniting. We need an immensely wider vision and viewpoint to give the conception its real meaning.

We are now conceiving that the 'I' in us, the incarnating soul and spirit entity, is an immortal being, returning to the school of Earth again and again to learn the lessons that each historical age can teach. If this be so, then we have the whole of eternity for the endless journey in spiritual and physical evolution.

Thus we may accept the binary viewpoint with much more confidence. Somewhere in the whole surge of life and being is an immortal droplet who is truly the complement to our own soul and it is seeking us through all our incarnations. If it could find us and consciously merge again into a oneness as we were in the primeval beginnings, then what joy and wonder it would be!

The questing magnetism of separated love re-uniting could be seen to be underlying much in the human story. Each twin will for ever be unconsciously seeking, and their longing search for re-uniting will at times be expressed in love relationships which, though great and beautiful, still do not necessarily imply the actual blending of binary souls.

Now it appears that, in our age, this eternal quest and its achievement and meaning is attaining an enhanced consciousness. Soul twins are actually finding each other. Those who achieve this age-long goal of blending into soul-unity, begin to recognize others who have done the same and to relate in what may well grow into a "binary movement". It could then prove to be a very vital aspect of the emergence of a new humanity, of which we have spoken in another chapter.

It should be recognized that the binary relationship, *as a conscious phenomenon*, is relatively new and is entirely significant as we pass the threshold into the Aquarian Age. Experience is showing that, when the step is achieved, it tends to bring a new certainty, joy and width of vision. This should obviously be so. Since we accept the possibility for soul and spirit blending, then we must recognize that our friend who has passed on, or our Higher Self, or even the Christ or Michael, or the God-source itself can speak *in our own thinking*. This truth and experience is of absolute importance. It is indeed the great turn-about in the centre of our consciousness. It implies a great step forward in taking personal responsibility as potential co-creators with God in freedom. Such is the ultimate purpose of our earthly incarnation.

The society we shall enter on the ethereal plane after we have left the body will be made up of relationships in blended thinking, for we shall then really be vortices of living vital energy, as beings of love and thought and will. We shall learn to lift and expand into the ocean of living intelligence and thereby take the vision and wisdom of the angels into our own consciousness, so far as we are able. How wonderful therefore if our soul-counterpart could re-unite with us now, balancing male and female and enriching our personality and comprehension. I stress again that this is not merely a case of close love-relationship, which may prove transitory. The idea implies a true blending and uniting of the two aspects of the original Soul Being, achieved *consciously* in our time after ages of unconscious search through many lives. Such understanding, be it repeated, could not have been fully understood before our present widening of spiritual vision and our accepting of a world-view recognizing the immortality of the soul and its repeated re-embodiment.

With the emerging of the spiritual world-view in our time the twinning of souls can become a factor of high significance in human experience, enriching understanding and width of sympathy. It is obviously different from marriage. Once the binary relationship is re-established the new person will be free to make richer relationships in friendship, love and marriage. But we must recognize that the achieving of the twinned relationship is once and for all time.

This phenomenon clearly has its important place in the emergence of a new humanity. And it establishes a condition which can receive the inflooding of the Christ Love now enlightening the Planet.

In that remarkable gnostic Gospel of St Thomas, Jesus is recorded as saying:

> *Logia 22*
> *When you make the two one and when you make the inner world as the outer, and the outer as the Inner and the above as the below, and when you make the male and the female into a single one, so that the male will not any more be a male and the female a female, when you put a single eye in the place of the many and a single hand in the place of hands and a single image in the place of all images, then you shall enter the Kingdom.*

And again:

> *Logia 30*
> *Wherever the two are one, I AM with them.*

And in *Genesis:*

> *And God said, Let us make Man after our own image. . . Male and female created He them.*
>
> **(Gen. 1.26)**

When I wrote my first two books of this Trilogy, *A Vision of the Aquarian Age* and *Operation Redemption*, I was avowedly interpreting a world-view and discussing ideas held by others. This third of the Trilogy has perforce to be something different. It must, as its title implies, be a record of personal exploration and experience. Perhaps this validates the title, for surely we are all, in different degrees of intensity, on the same Quest.

It is of course essential that we are very reticent about our own spiritual experiences. To speak about them may dilute and weaken their power. I must however state that I have personally experienced what I am now writing about in this chapter, and am prepared to affirm that my own twin-soul has descended from the ethereal plane and merged within my own heart. It matters not if others should treat such a remark as mere sentiment or wishful thinking. I know it to be a true and genuine experience, as of a being suddenly plummetting down and filling the heart with an overwhelming joy, love and energy. I foresee that many in our time will begin really to have such an experience themselves. Indeed it carries conviction! This fusing of soul-twins in heart and mind will be achieved where the deep and ageless bond is real and the two partners have attained to adequate experience.

Frequently (as in my own experience) one of the partners will have left the body through so-called 'death', perhaps through tragic circumstances. This, if real love has been established, will of course create the necessary and profound urge to re-unite, for such soul-fusing could not possibly take place without the furnace of deep love and suffering. This however will often be transformed into joy and total acceptance and a recognition that the events, appearing tragic and desperate, were in fact planned by our spiritual guides.

I need say no more about the personal experience now thirty years in the past, but ever present. This proves to be a central aspect of exploration into God. Our angelic guides and higher self do indeed stage situations for our life education!

Here is a poem which may speak to some of my readers. It is Anonymous.

> It is eight weeks beloved since you died
> You left the stiffening, inert lump of clay
> That was no longer you,
> And cried aloud in ecstasy
> And suddenly I knew

That all that we believed in
Lived for, told the world
Had at its smallest count
Some measure that was true.

It is eight months, beloved, since you died,
And out of my aloneness I have woven strength
To build anew;
For all there was of truth in our relationship
Had eddied, grown, intensified
Till with a clarion call it sounds at the far
    reaches of the world—
There is no death, no separation of the ways
If man to love prove true.

It is eight years, beloved, since you died
And for eternity a part of you
Is in its essence me.
I know you are, and in that certainty
Is woven all the fabric of my life.
Gone is all sense of urgency and haste;
For all time now our spirits meet in time.
Loving, we are no longer bound by love;
Heart of my heart, we've set each other free.

It is obviously very important that the binary experience is not confused with 'possession' in the negative sense, nor is it just to be identified with wishful thinking about a much-loved friend, or one-time partner in love or marriage. This is a field calling for careful exploration and case study. It is only now beginning to be recognized as a highly significant phenomenon. The initial group that has come together to share this experience is still small. Yet when it grows it could become a spearhead for a veritable new renaissance, for it should release a new and vital creativity, enhanced human capacity and fuller power of love and devotion. And, be it re-emphasised, it will enhance rather than inhibit or limit the power to love others. In this field there will be no jealousy and indeed many will go through life without others having any clue to the inner change and enrichment that has taken place. This, however, is likely to bring about a new courage, warmth, deep joy, tolerance, laughter, tranquillity, inner content and acceptance, with wider vision and sympathy. Irritation, that bane of a hurried and worried world, may be transformed into serenity. And, further, it will remove all fear of death, for we may hope, ardently, for the moment of full conscious re-union.

Finally, let us re-affirm that, since Christ is Love, we shall be creating in the heart centre a vehicle for His entry. *This* is the 'possession' we want! Since He is above and beyond the negative emotions, we may expect, with this Renaissance, a wave of sustained love for all life.

When two complements have become united, with one on the Higher Plane, he/she will bring an enriching of vision and capacity. Life together will become a heightened adventure, for the two have become fully united, while still maintaining identity. It is a love-sacrifice which enables the ever-present Christ-power to operate in the material world.

In this sense it is a home-coming. We have arrived. Heart is filled. There will be a gentling and a relief. We now know with absolute certainty that when we, the body-bound partner, are released, we shall merge in Light and be received on to the higher planes, fulfilled in love.

> *My true love hath my heart and I have his*
> *By just exchange the one for the other given.*
> *My heart in his and mine he cannot miss*
> *There never was a better bargain driven.*

Through the Sacred Site into the Creative Plane

AND I WENT FORTH into the night and found myself in a wild moorland. When dawn light came I followed a stream among rocks and heather and birch trees and a few Scots pine.

There was the spring and around it great blocks of worked stone, some still standing like monoliths. Clearly the place had been a stone circle and some sort of temple. A holy site and I could feel I had been led here mysteriously. But clearly my embodied self, using lower senses, could not see what had once been there.

So I left my body sleeping, like as one dead, and lightly I moved to the spring. But still I had in me the emotions and fears and sorrows of the lower self. These precluded my 'seeing'. So I made a ritual sacrifice of them and burnt them out on a little altar and scattered the ashes out on the dawn breeze. What was left was a little nugget of gold.

Now I began to see the subtle forms of that which was here before. There were great trees, a glade or grove. Their ethereal forms still stood where once they had grown. My subtle body could become one with their great trunks, their roots gripping down into the rock to stand hard against the storm, their branches lifting up in sublime gesture into the realm of levity, their green fronds bursting and reaching on to a yet higher plane and ever subtler vibration.

Then I saw plants and flowers and experienced the life of 'green', the image of Life, which could live in my soul. Then the stone circle stood perfected, protecting the sacred spring. That spring still flowed with crystal water as it had done through all ages. Now I was seeing it as it had been when this was a temple site. My vision was opened to the structures and the natural forms as once they had stood. I could see how the worn rocks and mounds were what was left of the ancient holy place.

I took my nugget, as a charm or amulet, and I moved into the colour, the archetypal green of life within the grass and fronds. My life united with that ocean of Life. And I could go into the colour that glowed in the form of the flowers, red into orange into yellow—the green of life, fading and lifting into blue and widening through the indigo darkness and into the delicate and holy violet. These colours filled my being which took them and blended them in the structure of Life, and I knew how the Life of Colour had expressed itself into the exquisite forms of the flowers. Beyond the violet I was touched by the tip of a cone of Light, golden light shot through with silver which came down and first touched the crown of my head, penetrating down till the whole body was bathed in effulgent light. I was within the cone which extended upwards indefinitely and was moving down to blend with the pyramid of darkness and mystery of the material world.

So now I moved through on to a higher plane of creative, archetypal activity. I was out on to this wide and wonderful area. Here were at work the archetypal Ideas which from the mind of God were the architects of the forms of nature, "the permanent realities of all Things visible in the vegetable glass of nature" (*Blake*). They were Being. They were Idea. They flowed freely into form and dissolved again. Here was great continuous and joyful artistic activity. And craft, the original craft of life and light malleable to thought. Here the angelic beings played with shaping glorious forms of light and dissolving them again. And I saw how when an idea was perfected, it could be passed on down into the Earth plane, to be manifested in solid matter. So those ethereal colours could be caught up into flower forms, trees or flashing birds, forests, buildings, mountains, glittering peaks and tiny delicate objects and animals with shining eyes.

Here was the archetype of true adult education. This plane is what we imitated in all we tried at Attingham College. Here was the archetype of our Creative Leisure Summer Schools. Painting, sculpture, metalwork, weaving and all the crafts. And music, shaping with sound to touch the soul: and poetry to use the word to express yet higher ideas and realms of vision. Acting to portray the human being as he/she passes through the vale of embodiment, lost at times, full of doubt and fear, but lifting again to touch the realm of God's Joy.

This plane of the archetypes is a reality. Here too is the Golden City, El Dorado. Move up into it. You will be accepted as a citizen, for you are blended with the golden light and the soul you show is cleansed from the dross of karma.

So you wear the seamless robe of light and are worthy to walk up the golden steps to the Square where stands the University. Adult Education—this was the great vision which fired Attingham, that great house used as a cultural centre for all.

And this eternal plane is there for the one who has cast off the "fears and sorrows that beset the soul". This is an endless plane of creativity, where all the arts blend in glorifying the creative urge, the source of all joy and wonder, the love which is the forging of a Oneness which penetrates down into the plane of matter. This golden light revivifies. It is Life, active, conscious of divine, and we human beings are the instruments for channelling it. And we break through now into that realm of gold.

Shed all. Let all go. Give over to God and walk into the creative light. Let the unicorn come out to you and touch you with its horn. You are qualifying to enter the University— *Universus*. Those who experience this breakthrough can bring it back with them to darkened Earth. Here is the Diadem, the Elixir. This plane is there and the sacred sites were all ritual gateways to it, for those souls which would sacrifice ego and achieve the One Thing, the One Desire to reunite with Wholeness, with God and the Divine that is within all things. So great is this goal that we may sacrifice all that bounds and bonds us to matter and personality. Here is the task of the adult education of the coming time, when we shall build a new heaven and a new Earth and the darkness and cruelty shall be burned away and washed away.

The gateway is through every sacred spot. And every spot is sacred. So, Go to! Our field of action is adult education and the Whole of Eternity is ours!

PART VI

*Operation
Redemption*

What makes
the World go Round?

THAT INDEED IS a splendid question. Lift your thinking into the 'holistic' world view. The Whole is Holy. It is not a dead mechanism. It is alive, a vast living Oneness, a continuum of consciousness Divine. It is illusion to think that it merely consists of an infinite number of separate parts, and that we, poor fellows, are isolated and lonely specks of consciousness unrelated to the rest of nature.

The effort we must make in our thinking is to step beyond the position of mere onlooker and grasp that our thinking unites us with the whole. There is a huge ocean of thought filling all ethereal space, infinite and eternal. It is the primal thought of God, from which all matter and form is derived, for substance is indeed frozen spirit. There is not really 'spirit and matter', but rather we must see that matter is condensed spirit. First comes the divine idea of things. God's thinking creates. What He thinks or imagines comes into being.

In the beginning was the Word, and the Word was with God and the Word was God. By Him were all things made. . .

So first comes the Living Ocean of Ideas. The strands of this ocean are Beings. These in their myriads are all integrally part and aspects of the thought forms of the Creator. But they become self-actuating. They are the archetypal Ideas of all Things.

Imagine a sea of ideas, all alive, surging, pulsating, moving and turning so that the picture is continually changing, the pattern metamorphosing yet always a unity—as in a kaleidoscope. You don't get a living organism in the middle of a dead mechanism. All is organism within greater organism. The turning point is a concentration point of energy in a vast field of energy called the Solar System. The Sun is the great energy source. Behind the physical sun that we see with our eyes and which warms our bodies is the Spiritual Sun, the focal point of activity of the highest beings, the Elohim, of whom the Christos, the Cosmic Christ, is the greatest. Look into the sunlight and see, rising within the soul, the image of these myriad beings all attributes of God's energy, and all singing to his glory and, of course, moving in majestic dance.

William Blake, that great seer, knew this truth.

> *"What", it will be questioned, "When the Sun rises, do you not see a round disk of fire somewhat like a Guinea?" O no, no, I see an Innumerable company of the Heavenly host crying. "Holy, Holy, Holy is the Lord God Almighty". I question not my Corporeal or Vegetative Eye any more than I should question a Window concerning a Sight. I look thro' it and not with it.*

How could the earth *not* spin? How can energy stand still? It must move and metamorphose or it would fester. All is in movement, from the globe of Earth to the spiral nebulae and to the whole galaxy—also an organism of Divine Life, perpetually spinning. It is all a great design and dance. And it is continually evolving, complexifying, lifting through metamorphosis of form, so that consciousness may be heightened and increased. Thought comes before form: Life comes before death; Death, in the sense of cold contraction from which life has been withdrawn, is a condition derived from life and resulting from its abandonment of the form. But in the compost heap the physical particles go through change, and the beauty of the flower becomes sludge and finally sweet smelling dark humus to receive the seed. The seed (usually also spherical), is the point of formlessness, or matter returned to 'chaos' which can therefore receive the inpouring of the archetypal Idea once more. And so the cycle of plant growth is itself part of the Dance of Life. Life always is. It never stops and cannot die. It perpetually changes in form but is always one. Life in no case can die. If it could, then God Himself could cease and die—which is absurd.

The outer forms in which it manifests can dissolve, break down, age, metamorphose, be destroyed, or rather their energy can be released and the particles dispersed and solid matter break down into humus, the matrix for more life to manifest. *Life never dies.* Life always moves. The Thought which is Life, which is Love of itself and of all, is eternal and changeless—it just IS and can say I AM THAT I AM. But manifested in form, it will perpetually move in a supreme cosmic dance, a great unending symphony as every form sounds out its own note or vibratory rate, each unique and together forming the 'music of the spheres', which can be heard by the inner ear of the mind.

For mind in man is an attribute of Mind in God. He creates our minds, and our brains are formed out of the convolutions of Divine Thought, so that they may give us working consciousness while we, as spiritual beings, are incarnated in the drastic limitation of the prison of the senses. But mind is a pulse of the Eternal Mind, no less. Step out in mind. Go inward to expand into the realms of thought, into Eternity. There 'see' that the turning Earth is merely a focal point of living energy, spherical inevitably as the expression of life, a body of substance which is secondary and derived from the unending dance of life. Earth is alive, an organism, of which mankind is an integral part. Our bodies are sensitized points of earth, our minds the link with the Eternal, outside time and beyond space.

Let all this sing in your mind. There is no death, no cessation of the movement of energy. I quote from Edward Carpenter:

> *There is no peace except where I AM, saith the Lord.*
> *I alone remain. I do not change.*

As space spreads everywhere and all within it moves and
*   changes*
But it moves not nor changes,
So I Am the space within the soul
Of which the space without is but the similitude and
*   mental image.*
Comest through, to inhabit me, thou hast the entry to
*   all life.*
Death shall no longer divide thee from those thou lovest.
I Am the Sun that rises upon all creatures from within.
Gazest thou upon me thou shalt be filled with Joy eternal.
Be not deceived. Soon shall this outer world drop away,
Thou shalt slough it away as a man sloughs his mortal body.
Learn even now to spread thy wings in that other world,
To swim in the ocean, my child, of Me and My love. . .

So to our question—how is it possible that the Earth should *not* spin to eternity in its endless dance of energy in relation to all the celestial bodies of which it is part, like a great organism? There is movement, there is metamorphosis but there is no death for Life itself, nor can there ever be. It is the illusion of limited brain-bound sense-bound intellect that there are separate things which die, that dead mineral comes first and 'life' is a chance and transitory development upon it.

Make the turn-about in consciousness to unite mind with Mind and know that Life and Divine Imagining was primal and is Eternal and its forms, being full of Living Energy, must revolve in Ethereal Dance, the Celestial Ballet.

Lift out of the temptation of 'reductionist' thinking. The Whole is *not* merely the sum of the parts. The whole is alive, in all its diversity and immense Unity. Thus (if you can take it) the heart is not merely a pump to push blood round. It is more like a *ram*, as in control of a dam or flood gates. The blood is the vehicle of the ego, and life drives it round, controlled by the heart in its rhythmical working. The ram does not drive the river along but controls the flow. And the heart is the organ for love, and the thinking of the heart is the vehicle for the Cosmic Intelligence which is administered by the Archangel Michael, Lord of the Cosmic Intelligence, Fiery Thought-King of the Universe, Countenance of the Christ, Wielder of the Sword of Light. In our age the sublime process is in action to convert this planet of Wisdom into a Planet of Love.

Towards a Spiritual Ecology

THE INTER-RELATED ONENESS of everything: Holism, Wholeness; the planet as a living being, an organism with its own intelligence, its own breathing and bloodstream of vital energies: the intricate plan and pattern of Nature as a work of art, a marvellous design—such concepts persistently flood into our minds. Not mere theory. Not a dogma for which belief is demanded, but a pressure of consciousness which penetrates and integrates our thinking with vision—the 'vision splendid' transfusing and lifting our thinking towards a light which, in its own being, becomes knowledge. This is a phenomenon now happening to us.

It is an *event* in the evolution of human consciousness. Look at it. In the last centuries, with the over-development of the left hemisphere of the brain, we have achieved splendid results in scientific investigation and technical civilization. Before us now is a great exploration of the mysteries of matter, but yet we have hardly touched the deeper meaning as to what it is all about. Why has the Earth happened? The common-sense basic mysticism of the enquiring mind revolts against the concept that it all happened by chance in a nature without purpose. So many now reach out for a spiritual world-view. As this rising tide of vision touches us and colours our thinking, we recognise that Earth is a living creature, that humanity is not the result of chance natural selection, but is in some sense the purpose of the whole divine experiment and grand design.

> *All are but parts of one stupendous whole*
> *Whose body Nature is and God the soul.*

So wrote Alexander Pope at the birth of holistic thinking. Such concepts must colour our understanding of ecology.

The green impulse, the wholeness thinking, comes to the rescue of a threatened planet. Human thinking in the last centuries of industrial man has been fired so much by the drive for profit. If a thing pays it is good. Gain and profit has become our god. The glaring example is, of course, the cutting down of the rain forests of the Amazon. This is happening now at 100 acres a minute and nothing, it appears, can stop this dreadful deed because it pays! Somebody makes profit out of it. And since the soil is essentially very poor, agriculture in that land will only be possible if huge quantities of artificial fertilizers are poured into it. But that also pays somebody very well! It matters not that by allowing this we destroy the great oxygen bank of the Earth and therefore bring about a deterioration in climate. How mad can we become? Our God is now Profit—and we shall have to pay for it.

Now emerges the holistic world-view and the realisation that humanity is integrally part of nature and is indeed the rightful steward of the planet. We have failed lamentably and culpably in our stewardship, but there is still time to redeem some of the damage we have done in our greed and avarice and ignorance— just time if we wake up now and change direction!

The wholeness thinking is lovely. It is humanity gearing in to the living whole of which we are the responsible organ. It is an awakening and brings the supreme hope of our time.

The 'Gaia hypothesis', put forward first by James Lovelock, is a dynamic inspiration reflecting the great truth. See Earth as a living creature with its own bloodstream, breathing and thinking, and see humanity not as mere onlooker, but as that point within the great design of Nature which has broken through into self-consciousness and so onward and out to cosmic consciousness. Thus we may see the burst of holistic thinking as an event of cosmic significance, a response within the human mind to the pressure of a dynamic universe of Intelligence.

Of course there is no need for a spiritual world-view before we throw our energies into conservation and 'wholeness' action. The steward of the planet takes up his true task of serving Mother Earth in the work of the Soil Association, the Men of the Trees, the Friends of the Earth, Wild Life Fund, Greenpeace and kindred ventures.

These noble movements are nourishing the life of nature and are turning the tide of human thinking towards true service of the threatened planet. No spiritual mystique is necessary for us to throw our support into ecological endeavour. The jargon of the elemental worlds, the angelic kingdoms and the power of the Spirit need not be brought in.

Yet how much more meaningful is our endeavour if we are able to see something of the scale of the spiritual world-view. It gives a majestic picture and ultimate hope, even certainty, about the human future after the cleansing of the polluted planet. The battle is now joined between the forces of destruction and those of transformation and redemption.

Think Wholeness. Realise that mind in man can encompass the Whole. We are that point where nature becomes self-conscious. Teach yourself the new way of looking at and into Nature.

The turnabout in the centre of our consciousness takes place when we recognise that every thing we see and comprehend with our senses has behind it and preceding its manifestation an original divine Idea.

Creation first involved the outpouring of the archetypal Ideas from the God Source, Creative Mind. The Ocean of Mind was composed of these great beings, strands of the Thought of God, who constitute the angelic realms. Then follows the miraculous process of transposing Idea into visible form on the material plane. Thus our imagination, as a faculty for intuitive exploration, can enter into tree, plant, bird, animal, crystal or cloud, and 'see' the living idea which animates it. This 'seeing' involves an enhancement of our normal looking. Mind is apprehending the archetypal idea. We discover in ourselves that Nature has created an organ within her own being, which can lift to consciousness the vision of the archetypal Oneness that lies within and behind all visible forms. The design of the divided brain in man opens this unlimited possibility for exploration into higher reality. The right hemisphere, more feminine and intuitive, is like a fountain, a spring through which can flow thoughts direct from Source. Obviously we cannot know what this flow of thinking is going to produce until it has flowed. Hence the importance of the two sides of the brain. Left hemisphere, the masculine intellect, is so designed that it can observe the bubbling fountain. Thus man can consciously 'think about thinking'. The potential is clearly unlimited. We are the one point in Nature which can undertake such exploration. It is the great adventure for the human being at the dawn of the Aquarian Age. And one can begin by gently teaching oneself to look into plant and tree and bird in such a way that we can apprehend the invisible pre-existent being within and behind the form. This is a love which unites us with nature and enables us truly to see that every form is integrally one with the whole, which plays in exquisite delight and artistry into every aspect of nature's totality.

The Oneness vision will open us to a science and technique for working with living Nature in love and caring, co-operating with the elemental beings whom the new consciousness can apprehend. With love that inevitably arises from this vision, we shall look with horror at what man is doing to living Nature for the sake of gain.

This is much more than airy theorising. It is a veritable turnabout in the centre of our consciousness, an emerging vision and energy flowing through humanity, reflected in the ecological and spiritual movements which constitute holism.

And it emerges now as a force, a rising tide, in the width of the 'Green' movement. Thus a recent Times article, primarily directed at the food business, spoke of the "Green consumer" or "Conscious consumer", realising that such a powerful body of people are now prepared to pay more if they can get good, organically grown food. The whole movement rides forward powerfully, bringing new understanding.

The very survival of humankind turns upon our awakening to the wholeness vision and beyond it to the spiritual nature of the Universe. Then the planet Earth is seen as the training ground for souls, the setting for a grand experiment in allowing a hierarchy of spiritual beings, "a little lower than the angels but crowned with glory and honour", to develop to freedom. The angelic world is not interested in freedom in the human sense. Angels are directly part of God Thought and their delight is to serve God. Man (male/female of course) is given freedom and therefore can develop as a son, a friend of God, a co-creator. Hence the obvious interest of the Higher Worlds in the destiny of this planet. If we disintegrate it in nuclear madness and war, it will damage the delicate balance of the galaxy. But here is the major paradox. The angelic powers are forbidden by Divine Order to interfere with human freedom. The fallen angels and beings of darkness have no compunction about taking us over by direct attack. Hence the vital importance of our grasping the concepts of spiritual ecology and the living wholeness of the planet. Once we dedicate ourselves in love of God and Life to service of the Divine Will, then, without any interference with freedom, they can flood us with their power.

So the battle for Earth is joined and we human beings are a vital factor for good or ill. Clearly things have gone so far that drastic earth-changes are bound to take place and many will die in the process. Die? but an essential aspect of the Wholeness Vision is the certainty that the 'I' in each of us is an imperishable Divine Being, a droplet of God, in training to carry the gift of free will. For this being there can be no death, for it is Life. When the body temple is destroyed by fire, flood or famine, that droplet of ego will be released to levitate to the soul groupings to which it is attuned. Hence the absolutely vital importance of what we are each attuning to NOW. Death holds no fears for those attuned to the Light. Those souls who have of free choice rejected the spiritual world-view, will still be alive after they 'die', but will be shepherded to some other planetary level for their continuing education and evolution. But what an opportunity will have been missed!

Thus to grasp a spiritual view of ecology in the service of Gaia and the living Earth is of major importance in these immediate years. Time is running out. The changes are upon us. Operation Redemption is launched and each individual must come to terms with the implications and the potential for good or ill. It is a free choice, calling for a new ecological vision of the living Oneness of Nature and Mother Earth, in a Universe spiritual in its essential Being.

GOD'S GRANDEUR

The world is charged with the grandeur of God.
It will flame out, like shining from shook foil;
It gathers to a greatness, like the ooze of oil
Crushed. Why do men then now not reck his rod?
Generations have trod, have trod, have trod;
And all is seared with trade; bleared, smeared with toil;
And wears man's smudge and shared man's smell; the soil
Is bare now, nor can foot feel, being shod.

And for all this, nature is never spent;
There lives the dearest freshness deep down things;
And though the last light off the black West went
Oh, morning, at the brown brink eastward springs—
Because the Holy Ghost over the bent
World broods with warm breast and with ah! bright wings.

(Gerard Manley Hopkins)

The Re-Dedicated Temple

THE HIGHER SELF SPEAKS:

Body is the temple which can receive the immortal droplet you call 'I'. It is beautifully designed and adapted for this descent of spirit down the scale of light-energy into the dense, slow vibration of the material world. Then your ego may of course get involved with desire, and can fall for temptation. The nature of the Divine experiment involves your having free will and therefore being permitted to err. The little local self is perfectly free to enjoy sensation, gratify desire, become possessed by lust, greed or fear. This is not the real freedom. It is illusory freedom, for it is really possession by impulses or beings who desire to drag humanity down into the mire of matter—into Hell, indeed. We on the higher plane must therefore watch and wait, since by Divine Command we may not interfere. Humankind is to be given freedom. Thus the temple becomes too often degraded and is used by the "money changers" and becomes the vehicle for gratifying desire. Then the Christ Being and the Christed Angels have to stand back, for they may not be contaminated.

Now you begin to see that your true task is to create a temple which can receive the Christ, the Lord. It is up to you to transmute the body temple, lift its quality of desire, metamorphose soul in such a way that it can be the receptacle for love and creative life, dedicated to service of the living spirit. The first temple we made for you, after long evolution becomes vehicle for receiving soul and Self.

The transmuted temple in which enlightened soul has been blended with the material plane, is to be offered by you for the descent of the Christed Beings and the Higher Self. Your initiative is, of course, the primary factor. This is your essential contribution to the redemption of Earth.

Every human centre which re-dedicates itself in this way begins to glow.

It is part of the enlightenment of the planet, which is growing luminous. This is an impetus spreading through the human layer, as one human being after another re-dedicates the cleansed temple. All so touched recognise each other and are drawn together in a new quality of love and tenderness. New dawn indeed, New Age arriving, new joy and companionship, friendship bound by united dedication to the coming of the Christ within, in light and power. So the re-dedicated temple becomes the vehicle for transformation and cleansing of the benighted planet. The plane of angelic being surrounding the planet, of course invisible to earthly senses, is poised in readiness to enter and take over wherever the human being in freedom re-dedicates self in service of the light. This is the great adventure of our age. Go forward with joy, to receive Him whose service is perfect freedom.

Look Within
for the Living God

Do not look for God outside yourself, for the God
*   which you seek does not exist.*
God manifests in us as light in our spirit,
Sweet warmth in our heart,
And strength in our will.
Look within for the living God, and be thankful.

Ask that God may live in you, that He may manifest
*   through you. Only God can transform human beings.*
Everyone is seeking the meaning of life.
The meaning of life lies in communion with God.

The Great Beings, Geniuses and Masters of Humanity
*   are those in whom God lives.*

God is the goal of life; it is He we are seeking.
God is the beloved of the human soul.

(Peter Deunov, the great seer of Bulgaria)

THERE YOU HAVE IT. This is the Truth. This is the goal. This is
the endless fulfilment of our exploration into God. This is
the experience of the home-coming. For this we are in incarnation
on Earth. God, the Source, is Life, everywhere. Wherever you
apprehend Life, there is God. You are alive. There is God in
you. Think to Him. Talk to Him—in your own lifted thinking.

So different is this from the God who is vastly distant and unattainable, who judges and metes out reward or punishment. Humanity had in its evolution to go through the phases of fear of a Jealous God and worship of the infinitely distant God. And even the doubt or denial of the existence of God. But now, as we cross the threshold into the Aquarian Age, melting and dissolving barriers, experiencing the rising tide of God-Love which seeps into all corners, trickles gently or washes away in irresistible flood, undermining all resistance; Now as conscious vision expands and we see that the being in us, the I AM in each of us, is a living, imperishable droplet of Divinity; Now when we grasp that Planet Earth is the chosen training ground and school of souls and that we have all been through and experienced all periods of history through repeated Earth lives; Now when we see that the whole of Eternity is ours to develop, evolve and perfect will and thought and the capacity to love; Now we can take this wonderful, tremendous, delicate and subtle truth—that God lives and speaks to us IN OUR OWN THINKING. Overcome the sense that you are too small and insignificant to call on Him and speak with Him.

Recognize that you are entitled as a human being to claim your Christhood and your Christ Light, for Christ is that aspect of the God-head, the Source, which is unconditional love. Indeed this is the watershed of evolution. This is coming-home for each soul that dares to take this step. "The endless goal is one with the endless way". We come home. We have arrived—but not at a stopping place. We move up the mountain and out of the cloud into the glory of vision of the great peaks. This is the achieving of the New Man, the fulfilling of this stage in evolution. The human being can step beyond the bondage to ego-desire and blend and merge into the totality of that vast Being which is Humanity. TRUE HUMANITY is in process of being born through each of us.

And the simple truth and experience is, be it repeated and repeated, that *God thinks and speaks in our own lifted thinking*. This is our direct contact. For this the human being and body was evolved over long ages—that there should be on Earth a creature who could think God's thoughts again, who could consciously grasp that risen thinking is the organ for exploring into God, that here within our thinking we can and may talk with God. We are entitled to do this. But we have got to discover it in our separate selves and have the courage to exercise this faculty. It is the sublime talent and divine gift.

Yet, since this is the Planet of Free choice and we are being called to become co-creators with God, the Higher World must wait on our initiative. An initiate is one who initiates. It would negate the divine gift of freedom if the angelic guides simply took us over. Then we should become automata of the Spirit. This is what Lucifer, the Light Bearer, thrown out from heaven for his attempt to usurp the throne of Christ, attempted to do. . . "Ye shall be as Gods".

The Planet at the entry to the Aquarian Age is to be cleansed and a New Humanity is to take it over. And each one of us is a responsible spiritual being, "a little lower than the angels but crowned with glory and honour". And, to say it again, this home-coming, this crowning event, this redemption lies in the discovery that *we can talk with God in our own thinking.*

We are to work at this. It is a path obviously fraught with danger of self-deception. It is a delicate and dangerous path. But we have the absolute certainty that we are closely watched over by our Higher Self and angel guide. These beings are outside our time scale. They are in ethereal space, beyond time. This implies that their response is immediate when we call on them. It matters not where they may be in the vast ethereal space. The spiritual being on that plane, whether angelic or your friend who has left the body, is *instantly* wherever he chooses to direct his attention.

Thus we are invited and urged to teach ourselves to work on our own thinking, to lift and prepare it as the instrument for exploring into knowledge of the Higher Worlds. We are *so close* to the spiritual beings who love us and are filled with the Christ Light and Love. But they are forbidden to constrain or take us over. They must wait till we call to them, of free choice.

Basically we are to teach ourselves to distinguish between the thinking which is involved with ego desires, anxieties, fears and ambitions, and the Thinking which is directly a vehicle for the Christ Thought. Both qualities are in our minds, the one like muddied water, often polluted and the other like a fresh crystal spring. We must learn of free choice to use the inner fountain, to cultivate a tranquillity and inner serenity, which cannot and will not allow criticism, doubt and fear, disturbance and anger.

> *If the Sun and Moon should doubt,*
> *They'd immediately go out!*

declared Blake.

Have the courage to reject doubt, and lift into a new integrity of thinking, a deeper certainty of soul. You can take the risk of self-deception, since you are always under loving guidance as you approach your true humanity. What matters is the motivation.

Act—Don't React

WHAT LIFTS THE HUMAN BEING beyond the level of the animal kingdom? We are designed to have freedom of choice. We are integrally part of nature, not a mere observer. The HU-MAN, a being of divine origin housed in the fantastically beautiful temple of the body, is the crowning point within Nature which has been given self-consciousness. The whole of Nature, integrated as a unity in all its complexity, is a wonderful design, a work of art. Planet Earth is the setting for this great experiment of the Heaven World, to evolve a point within Nature which can carry an immortal, divine, droplet and allow this to develop to the stage when it can make free, creative choices. It is as if the Almighty desired some setting within the Grand Design which could itself begin to be creative. Our beautiful gem of a planet is the setting for this extraordinary experiment. It was a risk, of course, for to give 'man' freedom implied freedom to err. Adversary forces and the fallen angels exploited this possibility, inflating egoism with desire for power (Lucifer) and denying the reality of the world of Spirit (Ahriman, Lord of Darkness). So we stand at the entry to the Aquarian Age, when the waters of the Spirit are being poured out to dissolve the old barriers and separation which characterised the Piscean Age.

So now, in our time, at the turn of the century, we are awakening in consciousness to see the task before us, the step we are called upon to take in becoming truly HU-MAN.

> *Let us make man after our own image.*
> *Male and female created He them.*

Free therefore to gratify ego desire or to take a great step in conscious direction and control of this organism in which we operate on earth. For this we must know—that the spark of Being in us, that which we can say 'I', *is* a droplet of God and therefore immortal and imperishable. For it there can be no death, for it is of God and 'God is Life', everywhere.

'We' are not our bodies. The body is a truly wonderful mobile temple which enables us, the true Being, to descend into the heavy density and slow vibration of the material plane and to sojourn there as an educational experience. Earth is a school for souls, and we are reaching a point when we can graduate to enter the "University". This makes our age so dramatic and exciting. It becomes a race between consciousness and disaster brought on us by our own ignorance, greed, desire, fear and folly.

So, to become truly HU-MAN, a conscious step must be taken in each human monad. In every situation involving decision, trivial or important, we are offered choice. Either we choose to gratify the desires of ego or we can select the course making for wholeness. Our understanding now tells us that we are each a facet of the Great Whole.

The animal world reacts to stimuli through the marvellous workings of instinct. Reflex habit patterns control the response. But think of the glory of a panther or tiger, and then imagine the creature let loose in Piccadilly at rush hour. It would be entirely lost and bewildered, since it would have no reflex habit-pattern for reaction. We are faced with comparable situations in the period of dramatic change which appears to be upon us. But the human being, each one of us, has its Higher Self and its Guardian Angel, very close to us and over-lighting all we do, staging situations for our training, but at the moment of choice standing back to allow us freedom to take our creative course.

With every decision we have the choice of reacting out of ego desire or into the course which makes for Wholeness. This latter course may draw violent protest from the ego, but it is the greater adventure, an exploration into our own Divinity. We are called on to *act* into our Higher Self, learning to take decisions for which we may have no pre-formed habit pattern or brain track. But there the recognition of the reality of our Higher Self is so important. This angelic being, a part of our nature, is ever present as guide and guardian, but it will never interfere with our freedom. It plans and creates situations for our testing. If we will choose boldly to act into the wholeness, ignoring the cries of disappointed ego, we shall begin to find that a power and certainty will be flooded through us. We are learning to co-operate closely with our Higher Self, and this is the great adventure in achieving our true humanity. Humanity is indeed in a pre-birth condition and we are now, in this calamitous epoch, waking up to the sublime possibilities which are held in store if we can awaken and work with our Higher Self.

Thus the primary task for each of us is to learn how to withhold reaction to a stimulus, thus cutting out all the old reflex responses which automatically follow when we react. It is a wonderful experience of freedom. There is no need to respond, to DO. So often automatic response is like a kind of possession. We are possessed by deep-seated old reactions built into our soul and psychology. These are cut out by withholding reaction. Then we can freely choose. Then each response could become a creative deed, in co-operation with the Higher Self. Then we begin to be truly hu-man.

No need to be worried as to whether we have really chosen the 'Wholeness' course. The Higher Self is so close that, if we get it wrong, it can pick us up, dust us down and start us again to deal with the next situation. Earth life is testing, trial, and training in a great school. Learning to act into the Higher Self is the noblest deed for man. It is the clue for living through times of change—and these are on us now! Thus the technique of teaching ourselves to withhold reaction, and then act by conscious choice is of paramount significance in this time. Grasp the idea. Work at it in daily life.

ACT—DON'T REACT

Closing Chapter
The Cosmic Pendulum Swings

I FOUND MYSELF in the Berlin Museum which houses the wonderful Pergamon Altar with its magnificent Hellenistic frieze of warriors and gods in battle. I was looking at the figure of Athene when further insight came to me. Here was the image of perfect human beauty, bodies in perfect co-ordination, intelligence of highest quality. But this phase was not a consummation. It was a stage, a step in a long story which continues through our own time.

I must simplify greatly in attempt to clarify a viewpoint of vital importance. What happened in the Greek culture was a phenomenon of profound significance—*individualised thinking flowered for the first time in evolution.* Previously 'thinking' had been the prerogative of the initiated priests, whose consciousness had been opened to the divine plane. It was the thinking of the gods reflected in the human mind. The consciousness of the uninitiated was nearer to that of the animal creation, under guidance of a higher world.

In our present age we are grasping the spiritual world-view and understanding that first from the primal Mind of God, the Source, was poured forth the ocean of Life and of Thought. First came the archetypal Ideas of all things. Blake expresses this truth so well.

> *This world of Imagination is Infinite and Eternal, whereas the world of Generation or Vegetation, is Finite and Temporal. There exist in that*

Eternal World the Permanent Realities of Every Thing which is seen reflected in this Vegetable Glass of Nature. All Things are comprehended in their Eternal Forms in the divine body of the Saviour, the True Vine of Eternity, the Human Imagination.

(William Blake)

Now back to the Pergamon Altar. Those marvellous sculptured figures showed the human body in perfect co-ordination, animated by mind and spirit of high quality and intelligence. but not a final and finished product. Nature is always in evolution. We are looking at a stage in which individualised thinking has awakened for the first time. Previously, as we have seen, the 'thinking' of man was essentially the advanced faculty of initiates who were open to the Weaving of Divine Thoughts. Now for the first time individual intelligence emerged within the human mind and it was experienced as a joy, an excitement. Socrates was teaching his young friends the sheer delight of exploring ideas in a self-sustaining ocean of Living Thought. Those famous Dialogues are not discussion sessions in our sense of the word. Socrates was leading the minds of his pupils through the fascinating labyrinth of logic—not dry, dead, academic logic but active experience of Thinking as an ever-flowing self-sustaining structure of Divine Ideas.

"Yes, indeed Socrates", "Surely, Socrates, that must be so!" "Ah, how right you are Socrates". Those young men, virtually for the first time in evolution, were experiencing the joy and delight of individual thinking, a nascent faculty in the human being. This was *not* a final condition, but the opening of an evolving faculty, as the ocean of Divine Intelligence worked down and out into the human layer.

We may follow this evolving process. This survey must be brief and superficial and not an academic study. I wish merely to establish the concept of the evolution of consciousness in thinking and the reality of the great ocean of Divine Thought poured out to mankind from the Source. Its bright April was in the great period of Greece. Under the Roman Civilisation we find this divine faculty taken for practical use in building up a great administrative and military empire. There were great philosophers and poets indeed but the fresh flowering of Thought in Greece had now evolved for practical use. Then the Empire was overwhelmed by the barbarian invasions and Europe entered a dark age. This however saw the growth of Christian establishment in church and monastery and the building up of a philosophic structure on the teachings of Aristotle. Out of it rose the glory of the Gothic cathedrals in an age of faith, the adolescence of a new Europe.

Look then at the Italian Renaissance. Here the human mind turned back to the classical days of Rome and beyond it of Greece. The Renaissance is too often treated as a discovery by man of himself and the world. The deeper truth is surely that, in this change of consciousness, man *lost* himself as a spiritual being, while waking up to the beauty of the world and the delight of exploring it.

Thus Copernicus and Galileo established that the Earth was round and was moving round the sun. It was not the fixed centre of the universe, and they could prove it. But the wiser members of the religious community could have seen that something tragic was happening. The price man was paying in discovering the secrets of Nature was to *lose himself as a spiritual being*.

Truth is found to be a variable commodity dependent on the world-view you hold. Copernicus and his followers quite rightly established that the spinning Earth revolved around the Sun, and that it was a tiny planet in an immense universe. Therefore the significance of man appeared to be 'debunked'. We are an unimportant expression of life in a tiny corner of the universe. But the wiser members of the church fraternity must have looked on with sorrow. The Copernican world-view, true on its own level, was jettisoning the profounder vision of humanity and its destiny. Man, they knew, is a son of God, first in creation. This planet Earth is the setting for a sublime experiment. Nature is a grand design, a wondrous work of art. The human being is the crown of nature, that point where nature becomes self-conscious and can look out into cosmic space and think God's thoughts again. This gem of a planet in all its beauty is the setting for the Divine Experiment in which Man can evolve to the point when thinking can in freedom reunite with Divine Thought.

Then the human being can, in freedom, become a co-creator and friend of God. It is a majestic picture of the purpose of life on this planet in a nature that is a work of art. Not chance natural selection, but a divine design. Seen in *this* perspective Planet Earth IS indeed the centre of the universe!

All this was thrown away in a world-view that limited truth to the mechanical workings of the material world. It is as if we are taken into the theatre to be shown the workings of lighting, accoustics, seating and setting of the drama, but rather pathetically we say, "but I came here to see Hamlet!" The meaning of the play is forgotten in the thrill of exploring the workings of nature. Inevitably Renaissance thinking led to a heightening of egoism and an intensifying of materialistic thinking. It is interesting to see that Renaissance art is almost entirely religious in its nature. It is as if the spiritual world wished through the artists to make the great affirmation that Man is essentially a spiritual being.

> *Remember this while you take the plunge ever deeper into the mysteries of matter. Your thinking is going to cut you off completely from the invisible world of spirit. You will lose all knowledge of what you really are. You will in time break through to a new Renaissance when you will rediscover your real nature and your place and destiny in the great divine design. Do not forget! Use your intellect to explore and control. Go through the pride and greed of egoism and desire, but, when you have plumbed the depths, then rediscover your true nature and start the great journey back to God. Your task is exploration into God. You will re-awaken. Your own intellectual science will become the vehicle for rediscovery of the Truth of God and the meaning of the design of which you are a crowning feature. Press forward into this New Renaissance which will lead you on and up into the Aquarian Age!*

Such was the message for all time and it holds good for us now.

It is also clearly implied in the opening chapter of Genesis, where God makes all things 'after their kind'—birds, plants, fishes, animals, each 'after their kind'.

And Man—"after His own image; male and female created He them". Then in Chapter 2 it is declared that there were no plants on Earth since it had not yet rained, so a second creation is described.

Clearly that little phrase, 'after their kind', implies the creation of the Archetype, the group-ego of a species, a high angelic being in the spiritual world, before any solid matter had been formed. In all its generation of these archetypal *Ideas* in their wonderful and rich diversity, together they always made a whole, each differentiated part integrated with all the rest in perfect balance and relationship. A complex spiritual tapestry which, when externalised into primal matter and substance, manifested as Eden Garden.

Here each emergent creature was naturally in harmony with all others. The fruits of the earth were there for the taking. Angelic beings (the Archetypes) moved and wove together in a celestial pattern which was reflected in nature. And Man, the Hu-Man being, male/female, found itself as natural steward of this earthly garden. "Be fruitful, multiply". The plane of the Archetypal Ideas, exalted angelic Beings, is of course still there and can be experienced by those with awakened vision, for the human being can lift and intensify thinking to move up into the realms of high solar frequency which overlight the material plane.

In imagination we can all lift and grasp this primal Oneness, the integration of all life into an inter-related vibrant Whole, held in the Divine Mind. Holism as a world-view implies that in our age the individual can with risen thinking experience again the ever present reality of this integrated realm of the Spiritual Archetypes.

In earlier cultures the priestly caste, the initiates whose

consciousness was highly evolved, could be in direct touch with the gods. 'Thinking' in Man was then a blending of mind with Divine Mind. It was a spiritual consciousness achieved by the advanced souls who could enter into the plane of Divine Thought. Lesser mortals, though evolved beyond the animal kingdom, would have experienced a level of consciousness below that of the spiritual thinking open to the initiated priests. They were taught by myths, legends and drama which enshrined the spiritual truths.

We have grasped that each animal species, 'after their kind', is controlled by a *group ego*, who is an exalted angelic being. Thus the archetypal Being of lion, swallow, bee, bull or eagle controls and directs every member of its species in all it does. This we call 'instinct'. The angelic archetype operates from a higher spiritual plane, invisibly overlighting the world of matter. In Man the individualised ego, as a spiritual droplet of divinity, descends right down into matter. Thus the human being is differentiated from the animal and becomes a creature that can think, decide and act out of itself. Earlier cultures are closer to the spiritual worlds and the manifestation of 'thinking' would have been a blending with Divine consciousness. For this some kind of initiation would have been essential.

Hold to this great thought—that the HUMAN ARCHETYPE is first in creation in the Divine Mind.

> Let us make MAN after our own image.
> Male and female created he them.

Thus the materialistic conception that man, since he emerges later than the anthropoid apes, is therefore the last in creation, must be rejected. Man, though last to appear in physical form, was there from the beginning as spiritual Archetype. With every incarnation we are each of us approaching nearer to the realisation of this archetype. Imagine what we shall be as artists, thinkers, lovers, healers or athletes when this stage is achieved! The full beauty and power of the realised Archetype was revealed in Jesus the Christ. It was nearly touched in

beings like Leonardo or Michelangelo. Facets of its splendour
are seen throughout history and in our own time. Here is the
goal of evolution standing before each one of us. We fell from
Eden Garden, the Innocence of the primal Oneness. In Blake's
phrase we pass from *Innocence*, through *Experience* and on to
Imagination, that condition when we have lifted back and up to
the New Jerusalem. This is the note for our epoch at the entry of
the Aquarian Age.

> *I will not cease from mental fight*
> *Nor shall my sword sleep in my hand*
> *Till we have built Jerusalem*
> *In England's green and pleasant land.*

Renaissance inspiration spread through Europe. Its flowering
in England is best realised in the cycle of the Shakespeare plays,
the burst of creativity in music, poetry and architecture and in
the towering genius of Francis Bacon. Then in the next century
the immense figure of Christopher Wren, in whom the balance
of the two hemispheres of the brain is fully achieved. So also in
Isaac Newton in whom intellect is perfected as an instrument
for exploring nature. Wordsworth, himself a scholar of Trinity
College, Cambridge, describes:

> *The anti-chapel where the statue stands*
> *Of Newton, with his prism and silent face.*
> *The marble index of a mind forever*
> *Voyaging in strange realms of thought, alone.*

Newton it appears wrote some two million words on aspects
of occultism and when challenged by Boyle for his concern with
astrology replied, to close the conversation—"Sir, I have studied the subject. You have not."

Yet with the 18th Century "Age of Enlightenment", the trend
of real materialistic thinking is established which, in the 19th
Century, manifests in our present scientific world-view. Hindu
mysticism sees this period as the Kali-Juga or Dark Age when
the spirit is wholly lost. It is now to be followed by the

emergence of a new Golden Age when the faculties of the two hemispheres of the brain, male and female, will once more be brought into balance and a spiritual world-view crown our scientific knowledge. Indeed intellect, which lost and denied the spirit, will become the chief instrument for its re-discovery.

This must also lead to the emergence of what is virtually a new sub-species of Homo Sapiens. It is a phenomenon of evolution that the step which Thinking takes is to activate the left hemisphere of the brain, the masculine analytical faculties, at the price of the atrophying of the more sensitive feminine faculties of the right hemisphere, which could enter the mystery of the living whole and apprehend the spiritual worlds. We should grasp the conception of Thinking as a Divine Phenomenon taken over by the left brain and used for analysing nature to satisfy the needs, desires and ambitions of Ego.

A word here about EGO. This little word implies the being which can say I AM, a droplet of Divinity, a spiritual entity as immortal as God is, but entering into embodiment as an education and training in the School of Earth. God Himself has declared I AM THAT I AM. The mystery which we have now to understand is that I AM IS GOD, a great being of whom every one of us is a pulse or fragment. Often we hear it said, in particular by Oriental teaching, that the ego has to be destroyed. The viewpoint of Western spiritual thinking sees ego as the indestructible being of man which indeed is to be transmuted and totally surrendered to God and Christ, but cannot be extinguished. It is that in us which can say 'I'. But of course it will be dragged down into egoism, poisoned by desire, polluted by greed, blinded by passion and lust, lured into darkness and delusion. This is the working of those beings who deny the spirit. We call them Ahrimanic, after the Persian Lord of Darkness who does battle with Ahura Mazdao the Lord of Light. Steiner first made clear that there were in reality two aspects of Satan—Lucifer who inflates egoism (Ye shall be as Gods) and Ahriman, the great denier of the Spirit. Faust's

Mephistopheles declares, "Ich bin der Geist der stets verneint"; "I am that spirit who always denies and negates". When ego has surrendered to these beings, it experiences the Fall. In our present culture both impulses are powerfully in action, creating a riot of confusion in our society. Yet we could not maintain our industrial society without Ahriman and his minions. They are at work wherever we see materialism in action—in a medicine that treats the body as merely physical; a psychology which denies the Higher Self; an astronomy which sees the stars merely as lifeless, gaseous bodies; a financial system which treats the making of money and profit as the primary purpose; an agriculture which fails to recognise the *life* of the Planet Earth and is prepared to exploit nature for profit through chemical processes. Thus Steiner for his centre at the Goetheanum personally carved the 30 feet group of the Christ Being, his raised arm controlling Lucifer in the air above, while below him among the tree roots Ahriman is held in his place. He called it The Representative of humanity.

Our task is to achieve a total transforming of our egoism so that the divine entity, the true ego in each of us, the I AM which makes us Hu-Man, shall dedicate itself, of its own volition, to the service of Christ. Then will come the transformation, for the angelic beings of the light can then flood our earth plane without interfering with human freedom.

This is the goal and purpose—that each human being may claim his or her Christhood, truly volunteering to be used as a channel for the inflooding of unconditional Love. Here we have touched the great challenge and hope of our benighted age. This knowledge shall be made glorious. Our personal I AM can be taken over by the Cosmic I AM, the Living Christ Power.

Now back to our thoughts about Thinking. The last three centuries have shown the descent into rational materialism in the Western mind. This implies an over-development of the masculine left hemisphere of the brain and, as a direct result, the atrophying or going dormant of the more feminine faculties of sensitivity and intuition in the right brain, which can apprehend the living whole, the totality of Spirit animating all creation.

The natural result of this imbalance is that the spiritual worlds have simply disappeared for us. No longer can we see the elemental beings in nature; no longer apprehend the angel guides and guardians who in fact closely watch over our lives. God himself is thrown into doubt and so agnosticism and atheism are common. Doubt and fear stalk the world.

But we are awakening to another factor of profound significance. Michael, the great archangel who overlights our present epoch, is known as the Fiery Thought-King of the Universe, the Countenance of the Christ, the Wielder of the Sword of Light. He is the Warrior archangel who fights for Christ as He overcomes the world. He therefore is closely watching all our lives, but he may not and will not intervene or take over until we wake up to his reality and call upon him, offering our whole selves as volunteers for his ranks. Thus we have each of our own volition to grasp and understand the reality of his presence and power.

Michael is known as the *Lord of the Cosmic Intelligence*. It is he who controls that vast ocean of Divine, living Intelligence poured out from the Mind of God. Intellect is a faculty of thought in the human brain. This has been highly developed in modern man. It is our instrument for controlling and exploring nature. It has led us to a state of near catastrophe. As Wordsworth wrote:

> *Sweet is the lore that Nature brings.*
> *Our meddling intellect*
> *Destroys the beauteous form of things—*
> *We murder to dissect.*

Now we are seeing where unbridled egoism using the power of intellect has led humanity. Disaster faces us unless a transformation and a cleansing takes place.

The Michael Mystery reveals another great event. Michael has released the Cosmic Intelligence down into the human kingdom upon Earth. This is in response to the descent of the Cosmic Christ into the life forces of the Earth, so that He is immediately with us, living in our thinking, enlightening our understanding, dwelling in the heart that has lifted ego out of the morass of desire, fear, hate and violence. Yet the Divine Decree has laid it down that there shall be no interference with human freedom by the powers of the Light. Therefore the redemption of humanity and the Earth turns on a sufficient number of human beings of their own volition awakening to the true situation and dedicating thought, heart and will to the redemption of our benighted planet. We must invoke the powers of Christ and Michael and their angelic army. We must in our thinking and with our understanding grasp that the Earth is indeed a living Creature with its own breathing, bloodstream and intelligence and that we are each a facet of Gaia, our Mother Earth.

Now grasp the tremendous implications. The pendulum of Time has reached its ultimate point and is now beginning to reverse its swing. We have seen how individualised thinking first awoke among the ancient Greeks and how through 2000 years and more it has developed as intellect which has increasingly taken control in a masculine way, for power and profit.

Now the Michaelic Intelligence floods the Earth Mind, while the unconditional loving of the Cosmic Christ floods the human heart wherever it can lift itself out of fear and doubt.

The Living Christ power is there in the immediate moment, NOW. That is the ever-moving instant when we can always contact the Divine. The satanic forces strive to bind us down to past and future—remorse and regret about past events and deeds, fear of what might happen in time to come. Oh, cut it out!

Be a channel for the cosmic Intelligence of Michael and the unconditional Love of the Christ. This is the human deed for our time.

> *O my Beloved, fill the Cup that clears*
> *Today of past regrets and future fears.*

(Omar Khayyam)

The reversal of the swing of the cosmic pendulum is not our decision. It is a phenomenon in which we mortals are victim or, by our own choice, instrument. It is the great event. The tide (to use another metaphor) has turned. We, flotsam and jetsam, are lifted with it. Again our choice is whether we are to be drowned by the rising flood or ride the crest of the Wave. We are each and all involved in this event.

Having reached an extreme point of intellect devoid of spiritual vision and bound to physical brain, our consciousness receives the rising power of the Cosmic Intelligence. Each human monad or module is given the chance to awaken to the experience that it is a tiny but real vortex of living, spinning energy, poised like the gyroscope or top, and still, so long as the life-energy is active. If that is withdrawn the top wobbles and falls. If maintained the vortex point interacts with the entire field.

Nothing now can stop the swing towards the coming Light and Love. But we are always free to reject it. The field of high frequency vibration penetrates all living things, bringing peace or conflict according to how the entity is attuned.

In this light-field no negative energy can survive. Violence, hate, self-seeking, greed, fear will perforce be expelled, unable to remain on the finer plane of fire, light and love. Yet free will has been given by Divine Decree to every human entity. Those who out of their own chosen impulse have achieved metamorphosis of soul, have rejected egoism, fear and remorse and accepted ego, the I AM, as the Divine Attribute, will lift into a knowledge that each is one with the marvellous Whole, that God is everywhere, the Life and Essence within each created thing. The marvel begins—that the human entity, active and creative, knows itself as a droplet which is One with the rising tide of Spirit, the Cosmic Ocean.

A great cleansing of the Planet is upon us. Nothing now can stop it. "Operation Redemption" has begun. Those who turn to the Cosmic Intelligence of Michael, who accept the unconditional Love which is the Risen Christ, would enter a field of high vibration which would give absolute protection against dark attack. That which is given over to the lower vibration of violence and separation, simply could not live in that high-frequency field. But Mind in each of us has free choice. Learn to maintain the high frequency, Love-light vibration and we are surrounded by an invisible field of force through which nothing negative can pass. But the moment doubt or fear are allowed in, the protective wall is shattered—(like Jericho at the sounding of the trumpets!)

So the task and the wonder is given to each. Within humanity on Earth arises a new force composed of all those souls which have accepted the Risen Thinking, the Cosmic Intelligence of Michael, to transmute the brain-bound intellect where Ahriman is so active. Humanity is being born into its Divine nature, but only those entities who have consciously and freely chosen can sustain the forcefield of light. Entry into this condition is, as has been said again and again, only in the NOW moment outside the time scale of past and future. NOW the I AM can operate. The I AM kingdom is being formed out of all souls who acknowledge their Oneness with the Holy Whole of God. Dedicated initiative and Good Will freely given is the passport. The impregnable castle walls will shatter if doubt and fear are allowed.

But those who learn to remain on beam in the sustained meditation or attunement which can be maintained throughout the waking day, will know by direct experience that they are God's children. They will be guided through times of change with inner certainty. They know that the Higher Self will receive them in the name and power of Christ.

Let us close this book with quotations from inspired and exalted souls who lead into the New Renaissance.

On! I have guessed the end; the end is fair,
Not with these weak limbs is thy last race run;
Not all thy vision sets with this low sun;
Not all thy spirit swoons with this despair.
Look how thine own soul, throned where all is well
Smiles to regard thy days disconsolate;
Yea, since herself she wove the worldly spell
Doomed thee for lofty gain to low estate:
Sown with thy fall a seed of glory fell;
Thy heaven is in thee and thy will thy fate.

Inward! aye deeper far than love or scorn
Deeper than bloom of virtue, stain of sin,
Rend thou the veil and pass alone within,
Stand naked there and feel thyself forlorn.
Nay, in what world then, Spirit, wast thou born?
Or to what World-Soul art thou entered in?
Feel the self fade, feel the great life begin
With Love re-rising in the cosmic morn.
The inward ardour yearns to the inmost goal;
The endless goal is one with the endless way;
From every gulf the tides of Being roll,
From every Zenith burns the indwelling day;
And life in Life hath drowned thee, soul in Soul
And these are God, and thou thyself art they.

(F.W. Myers)

The human heart can go the lengths of God
Dark and cold we may be, but this is no winter now
The frozen misery of centuries cracks, breaks, begins to move
The thunder is the thunder of the flows,
The thaw, the flood, the upstart spring.
Thank God our time is now when wrong
Comes up to face us everywhere,
Never to leave us till we take
The longest stride of soul men ever took.
Affairs are now soul size.
The enterprise is exploration into God . . .

(Christopher Fry)

THE END
(AND THE BEGINNING)

If you become Christ's man
You will stumble onto
Wonder after wonder
And every wonder true

**(Carved on the Durham tomb
of St Brendan of Clonfert
the Explorer, d. 577)**